D1375954

one man's suffering. ... psychiatric history which has not yet come to a clo... and which should shame politicians and the medical profession into action. Too many people are still living in psychiatric hospitals because there is nowhere else for them to go. Too many are still deprived of their basic civil and human rights. And like Jimmy Laing, too many people are still given psychiatric drugs and electric shock treatment without being consulted or informed.

Though he does not use MIND's terminology, Jimmy Laing's description of the inhumane treatment suffered by people with mental health problems is yet another piece of evidence to fuel MIND's campaigns for a better life for users of psychiatric services.'

Anny Brackx, Publishing Director,
MIND (National Association for Mental Health)

Dermot McQuarrie is a Producer/Director at Scottish Television where he has been responsible for the series *Weir's Way*. In 1979 as the presenter of *Scotland Today Report* his film crew were the first to get inside Carstairs State Hospital following the murders which had taken place three years earlier. Subsequently he was invited back to Carstairs to make a further programme on the hospital. It was then that he first met Jimmy Laing.

FIFTY YEARS IN THE SYSTEM

Jimmy Laing
and
Dermot McQuarrie

Published in
association with

CORGI BOOKS

FIFTY YEARS IN THE SYSTEM
A CORGI BOOK 0 552 13892 4

Originally published in Great Britain by
Mainstream Publishing Company (Edinburgh) Ltd

PRINTING HISTORY
Mainstream edition published 1989   BRN 78543
Corgi edition published 1992

This book was set in 12/14pt Sabon by
Chippendale Type Ltd, Otley, West Yorkshire.

Corgi Books are published by Transworld Publishers Ltd,
61–63 Uxbridge Road, London W5 5SA, in Australia by
Transworld Publishers (Australia) Pty Ltd, 15–23 Helles Avenue,
Moorebank, NSW 2170, and in New Zealand by Transworld
Publishers (NZ) Ltd, 3 William Pickering Drive, Albany,
Auckland.

Made and printed in Great Britain by
Cox & Wyman Ltd, Reading, Berks.

TO THOSE WHO SUFFERED

Contents

I

Perth

The Perth which I was born into on 3 April 1929 was a place of great class distinction. My family lived in a four-in-a-block council house with two bedrooms, a living room and an old-fashioned scullery. It was one of the council houses which had been built before the First World War. Across Darnall Drive there was a row of private houses and bungalows. The children from our side of the street were never allowed to play with those opposite.

I was the baby of the family. The eldest was John, then Cissy, Joy, May, George, Billy, Ronnie and me.

Even at an early age I was a loner. I loved walking on my own up in the hills and my other great joy was being with old people, even when I was only seven or eight. I well remember going down the road to see an old couple who lived nearby. I can see them yet – him with his top hat and her with a net veil covering her face. I used to go there on a Sunday and sing hymns with them. Looking back now I suppose I never really mixed with my brothers and sisters. I preferred to walk alone or play with other like-minded bairns. Whenever I got the chance, usually at weekends but also in the evenings during the summer, I would spend hours walking around the Buckie Braes and Craigie Knowes and, although not a million miles from the house, in my own mind they were a safe haven from my father.

My father was a harsh, heavy-handed man, unlike my mother who was gentle and, as I have always believed, was of a very different class from him. One lunchtime when I had stayed out too long in the hills and woods my brother George was sent to bring me home. He found me sitting alone in the woods too terrified to go home, knowing what fate would befall me. As we arrived home I was trembling with fear. My father was standing at the top of the stairs.

'You're no' going to beat me again, Daddy?' I cried.

'No, no, son. I've got a big bag of sweeties up here for you,' he replied.

I can always remember my mother saying, 'Jack, for God's sake, leave him, for God's sake.'

Like many times before, I was strapped by my father who used his heavy leather belt on me and then I was put to bed. The next day I still wasn't allowed out of bed and the wee chappie from next door, Arthur Peterson, would come round asking if I was coming out to play. 'Oh, he's not well today,' my mother would say as she didn't want me going out until the bruising had gone down. Arthur would leave comics and sweets which his mother had sent round. Although I never got the comics or the sweets I always felt that the neighbours knew what was going on and it was their way of trying to help.

Although my father was harsh towards me I tried in my own way to get him to love me and in the evenings, as he sat in his chair, I would comb his hair and try to help him in any way I could. But all this was to no avail. He also held an iron grip over the rest of the family and my brother John was especially frightened of him. John had started work as a butcher's boy and as one would normally expect he wanted to go out on a Saturday night with his friends, but Father would have none of it. It was the same with the girls. We were virtual prisoners in the house.

My mother was very different from my father. As I mentioned, she came from fairly well-off stock. They would be called middle class today. Her family all had businesses, lived in lovely houses and one uncle had a car – quite a thing in the Thirties. Their children all had beautiful clothes while we had to make do with hand-me-downs. Even in those early years I wanted better for myself and felt that I should have nicer things. I always felt that my mother had married the wrong man. She was a gentle, beautiful woman whereas my father was a tyrant and a bully. She cried a lot when my father and she would argue and shout. Unlike today, when parents talk more to their children, we never seemed to have the chance to confide in her. She was always working and when she came home my father would be there.

Life for her was one big struggle to find money to clothe us and feed us, but she tried to make life a bit easier for all us children.

Many times after she and my father had had a particularly violent argument she would put her hat and coat on and come into our bedroom, kiss us all and say that she couldn't stand any more and that she was leaving. How we would cry when that happened! But in the morning when we got up she would always be there. Even though I knew that she wouldn't leave us there was always a thought that this time she just might. Listening to them argue, I often thought that if she and I could both leave then we would have a much better life together.

My most vivid memory of the treatment my father meted out to her happened one Hogmanay. A week earlier we had all celebrated Christmas. We had had the joy of getting up on Christmas morning with the anticipation of seeing what Santa had put in our stockings. Rushing into the living room we found each stocking filled with fruit, sweets, a game like snakes and ladders, a small toy and usually a threepenny piece. Although not much by today's standards it was a delight to receive these presents. As midnight of the year 1937 approached we were all getting the house ready to see in the New Year. All of us were allowed to stay up that night. After the 'Bells' we went downstairs to Jeannie's, our neighbour's, house. As the night progressed we couldn't find Father. My mother went off to find him and discovered him in bed with Jeannie. She came back into the sitting room and said to Sandy,

Jeannie's husband, a docile soul, 'Why don't you and I do the same?' But she was only wanting to pretend so that she would seem to be getting her own back at Father and teach him a lesson. Eventually Father came through and went looking for Mother. When he found her in the other bedroom he yelled out, 'What the fucking hell's going on here?' and ripped back the bedclothes – only to discover that my mother was fully clothed, as was Sandy. In his drunken rage he struck my mother.

We then went back upstairs and Jeannie and Sandy followed us and as soon as Mother was in the door Jeannie started playfully pulling at Father and tried to make a joke of the whole thing. I found it all very upsetting. Why my mother didn't leave after that incident I'll never know. From then on their relationship got worse and sometimes I'd find her in the scullery crying her heart out. But even then when I would ask her what was wrong she'd reply that it was nothing, that she just had a cold.

When I think back, what a life she must have had. Putting up with my father, struggling to raise eight children and then having to cope with my problems. I was what would be called today a 'problem child'. For no apparent reason I'd fly into a temper and have a tantrum, screaming and shouting. While I remember having these tantrums at an early age, they seemed to increase after my operation. I had a cast in my right eye and it was diagnosed as spondylitis and I had to have an operation at the top of my spine as the tissues at the top of the vertebrae were rotting away. While it helped rid me of the cast in my eye I still have a reminder of the operation to this day. While I was recovering from the operation in hospital I was lying face down on the bed with a cage over me which had electric bulbs inside it. This seemingly helped the recovery. Unfortunately one of the bulbs had rested on my hip and I remember that it was a nurse who discovered it while I was still coming out of the anaesthetic. It was reported and my mother's friends all said that she should sue the hospital. But Mother said she couldn't do that as the operation had been done for free. That was typical of my mother.

I can't think why my tantrums should have increased after the operation but they certainly did. Perhaps it really was the build-up of pressure on me, what with my father and all that was going on around me. These tantrums were not confined just to home. At school I had been happy during the first couple of years, first in Miss McLeod's class and then in Miss White's. When I moved up to the next year I became a real handful for the teachers. Perhaps today I would have been diagnosed as hyperactive but in those days you were classed as a problem child. No-one tried to study my behaviour or find out what was behind my problem. Thank God, today it seems that adults are more aware of the problems facing children.

At home I would stand out in the street and scream that I was starving. Of course the neighbours would all hear me. What an embarrassment it must have been for my mother. Eventually I was moved out of Craigie School to a 'special' school on the north side of the city. There we would play games or sit around in groups. Again no-one tried to deal with the problem. As I was to find in the ensuing years, those dealing with people who were in any way disturbed knew little or nothing about the person nor did they try to find out.

My tantrums continued, with the added pressure of my now being away from even my former schoolfriends. At home my father had gone to join the Army as the threat of war approached. Although I hated my father, when he wasn't there I really began to take advantage of my mother. I would pester her, probably at all the wrong times, and when she didn't have time to spend with me I would fly off the handle. I would even go and see her at her work on a Saturday which was obviously the last thing she needed, to have this little boy hanging around the shop causing her no end of trouble when I shouted at the top of my voice.

Eventually I was taken to see the school doctor. My mother told me that I was going to a place to stay. It had got to the stage where she could no longer cope with me, although she herself never told me that. I was actually happy about the prospect. It seemed like an adventure and, with all the problems which surrounded me at our house, I was glad to be leaving. Three weeks after seeing the school doctor we left the house early one morning, went by train to Dundee, got the bus to Dowanfield and walked up to Baldovan, an institution for disturbed children.

2

Baldovan

My mother and I didn't say very much on the journey from Perth to Baldovan. I was still very excited about going away but this was all to change within hours of my arrival there.

Baldovan, now known as Strathmartin Hospital, was reached from a large drive. At the time it was a beautiful day and I was impressed with the gardens, woods and even the buildings themselves. We arrived at the main administration block to be met by the only doctor and I remember his words to this day: 'Come in, James, you're going to be very happy here.' How those words haunt me now. The entrance hall, with the Superintendent's office on one side and the Matron's office on the other, had a beautifully polished floor and was decorated with various pot plants in brass containers, but through the doors the reality of Baldovan existed.

We went into the Superintendent's office and the doctor told my mother that they would take good care of me. She began to cry and then said goodbye. I must admit that this didn't upset me at all as I was still excited at the prospect of staying in what looked like beautiful surroundings. I was led down a long bare corridor and made to sit in a large reception area at the bottom of the main staircase. There, six benches arranged around a fireplace were the only furniture. I was taken away and bathed and put to bed. That night I cried my heart out. When I compared the surroundings of my ward with the 'government green' walls and 'government cream' ceilings and the whole place smelling of Izal disinfectant to that of the entrance hall and the Superintendent's office with its decor and plants where my mother had last seen me I suddenly realized where I was. As I looked around the dormitory with every bed with its institutional red bed cover I thought, 'Oh my God, what's going to happen to me? Am I ever going to leave here?' I was only nine years old. Even as young as that I was now aware that this was not going to be the delightful, beautiful place I thought I was going to when we had left Perth.

My dormitory was one of the smaller ones with sixteen beds. There were others which had forty beds and one which had sixty. They were just bare dormitories with highly polished floors. There were no lockers as you had no possessions of your own. You kept your pyjamas under your pillow. The windows had no curtains but they had blinds for the wartime blackout which were screwed into place and there was a small table in the middle of the dormitory where flowers were placed at ten o'clock every morning and taken away at four in the afternoon – regular as clockwork.

The daily routine began at six-thirty. You came down the stairs and stood in a row outside what was called the sink room. There was one toothbrush to clean everyone's teeth. There was a large bowl of tooth-cleaning powder into which the nurse dipped the toothbrush and then cleaned the boy's teeth. She would then rinse the brush out and proceed to clean the next boy's teeth. One brush for sixteen boys. There was only one towel for drying everyone so you quickly learned that the best place to be was at the front of the queue.

After washing you walked in line to the main reception area at the bottom of the stairs and sat with your arms folded waiting for the bell to ring calling everyone to breakfast. Everything was done to the bell. You daren't move until the bell rang. Mistakes in this area were rewarded with a slap around the ear. There was always an older boy put in charge to keep order because there was only one nurse on duty at that time. She was the night nurse whose duties included the sink room in the morning. Before going in for breakfast the incontinents were dealt with severely. If you wet the bed you were given a hammering. For this two or three of the older boys held you over the bed while the night nurse administered the hammering with a sandshoe. It was said that the reason you got the hammering was that she would have to report the incontinence and she took it as a slight on her nursing that she hadn't got you up during the night to urinate. No-one was excused. Incontinence was not to be tolerated. Even the little ones of three or four and right up to the eldest in their twenties were punished in the same way.

When the bell rang we all marched into the dining hall, saluted each member of staff and stood at the tables where we all sang 'Each day I rise'. Breakfast consisted of porridge and one cup of tea. If you were over fifteen you got a second cup of tea. You also had half a slice of bread. Lunch consisted of soup and pudding. The soup, invariably potato soup, was served from a huge great bath. The pudding was very watery. If you got a potato in your soup by luck and your pal opposite didn't he'd begin kicking you under the table and saying that you must be nurse's pet. At night-time you got two slices of bread and jam, one slice of bread and butter and a cup of tea. On Thursdays we had tripe and on Sundays we got a pie. There were never any meals with meat apart from Christmas when we had mince and tatties. Twice a week we were given a Paris bun. We were always hungry.

After breakfast we all stood and sang 'Praise God from whom all blessings flow' then formed two lines again, saluted the staff and marched out. Then it was time for work with the older ones scrubbing the corridors and the toilets while the rest of us went up to the school. The school wasn't a school in the true sense of the word. Today it is called 'occupational therapy' but we were doing something similar early in the war – sewing, knitting and painting. You returned from the school for lunch and dinner and on arrival back you removed your boots and walked about in your stockinged soles. No slippers were ever issued.

Our hunger was alleviated by the food parcels which the parents sent in. These would be opened by a nurse who took them from the large general cupboard in the sitting area, usually after tea at about five-thirty or six before we were put to bed. She would call out your name and you went and asked her for some of your parcel. Unfortunately some laddies didn't get parcels so some of us would share ours with them. Others, though, were very possessive about their parcels and wouldn't share anything. After this we went upstairs to the dormitory and before going to bed we all sang 'Now the day is over'. Bedtime was seven-thirty.

The only time you got something tasty to eat was if you were selected to work on the farms. From time to time they would pick two or three boys to go and work on a farm called Tod Hill in Ayrshire. It took in boys from institutions and also used to take children from the Quarriers' Homes in Bridge of Weir. But it was simply cheap labour. They also took groups to local farms near Baldovan. When you were on farm work you were given jam and cheese sandwiches for lunch and they certainly tasted much better than our usual daily soup and watery pudding.

About eight-thirty in the morning a tractor and trailer would come and collect us and take us to the farm, usually Powery Farm, Emmick Farm or Baldovan Farm. You would spend the day spreading dung or harvesting turnips. For this the laddies were paid in cigarettes, a couple in the morning and a couple in the afternoon. You weren't supposed to take them back to the institution but we always nipped them and then at night back in the dormitory we would share them, blowing the smoke out of the windows. But it really was cheap labour. You could be on that turnip field for up to twelve hours. The institution charged the farmers for our time and when you consider that it wasn't just one squad but that there were always quite a few on three or four farms, the money must have been a considerable amount by the end of the harvest. But we didn't receive any of the money. We reckoned that it was actually going into someone's pocket back at the institution.

I knew the whole arrangement was wrong. Even in the early years I said that this wasn't right, it was no way to treat people. But it has to be remembered that they really had no idea of how to treat mental problems. For instance the nursing staff weren't trained as they are today. There was no requirement for 'O' Grade or similar qualifications, for example. When you joined a hospital the way you became a staff nurse was that following selection you attended lectures upstairs in the hospital. You learned everything you needed to know from one book called the *Red Book*. That, on the male side, coupled with being tall and big, gave you all the qualifications necessary. If the doctor or the Matron liked you while you were attending the lectures then they would say, 'Aye, he'll make a good nurse.' But usually the real 'good' nurses were those on probation and in some cases their probation seemed to go on for years.

While Baldovan was a harsh, uncaring regime there were a few good people who worked there. I have fond memories of one. Catherine was like a mother to me. She even took me to Dundee on her day off. I became very attached to her. Out of the blue one day she wasn't there. I asked around for her and I was told she was coming back in a few days. She never returned. I found out much later she had returned to Glasgow and had had a baby. It set me back a bit when she didn't return but it was typical of the authorities at Baldovan that they didn't bother to tell me what had happened and give me some help. Of that period I would say that there were only a few nurses who were kind and warm-hearted towards us. The others were quite prepared to keep up the harsh regime. I can see them to this day in their starched white uniforms and flat shoes stomping about the institution. Another kind one was a gentle young soul who came from Wales. During the war when a nurse came to work in a hospital she wasn't allowed to leave unless she was going to another hospital. One day I found this nurse at the top of the day room. I asked why she was crying and she replied that she wanted to go home. I thought, that makes two of us. I told the senior nurse on duty that she was crying and they brought the doctor down. I can always remember it. They gave her two tablets and told her to settle down. They had no feelings even towards their own.

As far as the other patients were concerned, there were very few, like me, who could cope with the situation on a day-to-day basis. There were all types at Baldovan – not just working-class people, but businessmen's sons, a lord's son and a professor's son to cite just a few. The professor's son would sit all day in one place. His one great delight was cheese pie. But sometimes the other laddies would tease him saying, 'No cheese pie for Scotty today.' This would make him very angry. You have to understand that mental defectives, just like 'normal' human beings, enjoy teasing people but in their case you daren't get caught at it. The mental defective always wants to be of good report. He will give anything to be of good report. The thing he likes most is being told, 'You're a good boy, Jimmy.' So you'd ask the nurse if you could sweep the room and then you'd get a good report. It was unfortunate, though, that you had to sell yourself this way but that was part of the system.

The highlight of life at Baldovan was the visiting day. It was on the first Saturday of each month from two till four. The nurses would come round and for that short period before visiting they were all sweetness and light. 'Mummy coming today, is she? How lovely for you.' Bastards, I thought to myself. How cruel. We were all done up on visiting day in the regulation two-piece suit with our hair brushed. For hours before visiting we would stand at the windows overlooking the drive waiting for them coming up the hill. But while we all got dressed up, not everyone got a visitor; it was very sad to see the expectant faces drop when no-one arrived for them.

But to be fair to mental defectives there is always an air of optimism about them. They don't suffer for long. They really don't understand what is happening over a long period. They would say that their mother was probably busy today and she'll come next time. For some there never was a next time. I, on the other hand, was affected much more than others when I was told that my mother would be coming and she didn't turn up.

Another quirk of visiting day was the lack of bells ringing to announce what we were to do. In normal circumstances if you ran out of the day room without permission you would be greeted by, 'Where the hell are you going, Laing?', but on visiting days as soon as you saw your visitor you were allowed to run down the drive to meet her. During visiting the nurses and the doctor would be around saying sweet things to you and patting you on the head. In those days I did not know the meaning of the word 'façade'. I do now. Initially I put on a show for my mother. I didn't want her crying. Mum would give me the bits and pieces of news and I'd play along with the doctor's pretence when he told my mother how good it was here. But later on I'd begin pleading with her to take me away. Yet in all this I never told her about the hammerings or other punishments which were dished out. I don't know why. Maybe I felt that she wouldn't believe me and I didn't want to cause a rift between us. More likely I didn't want any

25

repercussions from the nurses if my mother had complained. Fear is one of the most powerful and torturous things throughout institutional life. As far as those in charge were concerned, visiting time was the period when they put on their act. When a child is in an institution those in charge are always seen to be in the right. A mother or father can talk to a doctor about the child and by the end of the conversation they'll be sent away thinking, 'He's right enough, that doctor.' Because people were so unaware of the many aspects of mental illness they always took the doctor's word for it. Towards the end of the visiting time you could feel the tension in the air as the patients knew that their parents would soon be leaving. There was a lot of crying.

Once visiting was over we immediately had to change back into our everyday clothes. I always felt it would have been nice to let us keep our good clothes on until it was time for bed.

Mother's visits eventually stopped. With my father away at the war she had fallen in with a chap who was manager of a bar next to the Queen's Hotel in Perth. They went off together to a hotel in Cornwall, she as housekeeper and he as chef. I did meet him once briefly when they both came up at visiting time. He was sitting on the grass and Mother introduced him to me. While first impressions aren't always the best I felt that she was not doing any better than she had done with my father. He seemed a dislikeable type of fellow. By this time also my brothers John and George were in the Army and May had joined the ATS. Cissy,

Ronnie and Joy were all dead. Ronnie had died when he was a toddler; Joy, when she was eleven or twelve; and Cissy died of scarlet fever in her teens.

For a while Mother continued to write when she could. She also continued to send me my weekly parcel.

My father visited me once. It was one evening after we had gone to bed. What a privilege it was. It was these little things that caused great excitement at Baldovan. 'Jimmy Laing's been let out of bed! His father's here,' was the whisper round the dormitory. I went downstairs and I remember my father walking in dressed in his uniform. I just looked at him and said, 'Hallo, Dad.' He handed me a big bag of sweets. I was anxious to get away. The visit lasted about five minutes. I can't say it affected me either way. Even when my mother visited we never spoke about him.

While Baldovan was an institution in the true sense of the word it wasn't a closed hospital. Indeed, it was so open that it was very easy to abscond from it. It was a regular occurrence for a group of five or six of us to run away. Sometimes we'd go off in twos or threes but mostly I went on my own. There was nothing planned about it; it was always on the spur of the moment. I invariably managed to reach Perth. Sometimes I'd hitch a lift with a lorry or I'd go on a bus and tell the conductress I'd forgotten my fare and she'd let me travel free. You would decide, say, in the morning, that you were going to abscond and you would work out the best time of the day to go. Playtime was the best. The big playground had the Emmick wood right behind it. You'd then tell someone you trusted. I had only one pal whom I could trust and sometimes we'd both go, and then you'd be off. Certainly the first time I went my heart was pounding with both fear and excitement. When I got to Perth, which I think was no mean feat for a twelve-year-old, I'd just wander around. Mother was away by this time but I had an aunt; I think she wasn't a real aunt but we all called her that, and I'd go to her house. She knew I'd absconded and she would give me something to eat and then say that she would have to take me down to the police station which at that time was in Dee Street. The police would then phone Baldovan and they'd send someone down to collect me. The police were very good about it. They never locked me up and I usually spent the time sitting in the police rest room with a cup of tea. They always sent the same person down: Pa Broon, as we called him. He was the head gardener. He always had some Woodbines with him and he would give you one. Then he would say, 'Now, you're going to be a good boy, Jimmy, and not run away from me.' That was because he knew that he wouldn't be able to catch you as he was so old. We never let him down. Other times when I would abscond with my pal we would be away for maybe twenty-four hours and then because we were starving we'd go to the nearest police station and give ourselves up. We knew that they would give us something to eat and a cup of tea.

When you were returned to Baldovan the doctor would be standing there with his fingers in his waistcoat looking very stern. He never asked why we had run away; all he would say was, 'Send for the chief engineer.' He would arrive and we would be led away for the 'treatment'. The chief engineer was the only one who administered the 'treatment'. Pa Broon refused as he had boys of his own about our age. You were led away to the room where there were four large baths which had overflow drains surrounding them. The bath would be filled with cold water and you would be stripped, a towel placed round your head and you would be dunked in and out quite a number of times. You were then brought out and made to stand shivering while you dried off. No dry towel was given to you and you did the best you could with the wet one. When you were dry you were taken to a little surgery just off the bathroom and given an excessive purgative called Crutin Oil. It was in a long-stemmed glass. The worst thing was that you had to take it mouthful by mouthful. As with all bad-tasting medicines you wanted to get it over quickly. I would say that there were about five or six tablespoonfuls in the glass. I was lucky, if that's the word, I was able to get it over. Some couldn't keep it down but they had to take it, no matter how long it took. You were then sent back to the dormitory and needless to say you were on the toilet for the best part of the next week. The end result was to weaken you. In the bad old days they used to hit mental defectives to get the 'badness' out of them; this was the modern-day version of the same treatment.

You also lost your porridge in the morning and you lost your suppertime slice of bread. You were also sent to bed early. The worst time was in the summer when you'd be put to bed at three in the afternoon while everyone else was out playing in the good weather. And yet knowing all the consequences I kept running away and got the 'treatment' every time I was returned to Baldovan. In those days there was no redress. It was to be many a long year before that came about. I did try to complain once. I had been incontinent for the first time in my life. Each morning the night nurse checked every bed in the dormitory. If you had been incontinent your name was called out and then you were given the kind of hammering I have previously described. I ended up all bruised down my right-hand side where the nurse had hit me with the sandshoe. I had never been incontinent before and I thought, 'I'm going to do something about this.' So I took the bull by the horns. At one o'clock each day they had surgery time, usually dealing with abrasions, cuts and boils and such like. For some reason the nurse who had administered the hammering was in charge of the surgery queue but as I had decided to complain I had to go ahead with it. When it was my turn I loosened my braces and went into the surgery.

'Well?' said the doctor.

I dropped my trousers to show him the bruises. 'I got these when I got a hammering for being incontinent.'

'Get out of here now or I'll do the same to the other side,' growled the doctor.

Once out of the door the night nurse grabbed me and told me that if ever I did that again I'd be really sorry. At that all the pent-up frustrations from being wronged exploded inside me and I let rip with a torrent of abuse and curses at the nurse. Naturally I was packed off to bed but then, out of the blue, a few days later I was told by another nurse that I was to be 'promoted' to Pavilion 5 from Pavilion 2. It really was promotion. The building was more modern, for a start. I was moved because they thought that if they let me get away with that kind of behaviour then everyone else would try it. I was delighted, though, to be away from that particular nurse. Sadly, while the routine was supposed to be different it wasn't. The nurses there tended to pick on the same type of people as was done in Pavilion 2. It was invariably the sixteen-year-olds and always the low-grade mental defectives. One case was with Johnny. He was a well-built laddie about sixteen or seventeen; a great worker who went out to the farms every day. Always clean and tidy, he was very good-natured though he had little reason to be. He was one nurse's constant whipping-boy. Madame Plump, as we called her, took great delight in winding him up and then when he would react she'd slap him about the head. One particular morning we were all in the boot hall waiting to go out to the farm. In comes Madame Plump and Johnny, who knew that he was going to get slapped by her, says,

'I'm not going to take this today. I cannae take it any more.' As she approached him he got up off his seat – I can see him now – and punched her on the chin. Madame Plump fell back but as she got up she took out a packet of cigarettes from the pocket in her uniform and threw them at Johnny. 'You're all right, Johnny, you're all right,' she screamed. She never hit Johnny again.

While my own case and that of Johnny's serve to highlight how you could put one over on the staff, they would invariably exact their revenge.

I continued to abscond at regular intervals and was always brought back and given the 'treatment'. Yet, that didn't deter me. I wanted to be in the outside world where I felt I belonged. Following one absconding I returned to find that the doctor and the assistant Matron were missing. They had been having an affair for many years. He had a family down the road but used to spend nights at the hospital, no doubt on the pretext that he had to treat some patients, with the assistant Matron. So instead of being brought up in front of the doctor I was met by one of the new auxiliary nurses. Just as he was about to mete out yet another hammering in walks Dr Robb who had been brought in to replace our Superintendent Doctor. The auxiliary immediately changed tack and said, 'Sit down, Jimmy, and tell me why you've run away again. You're an awful laddie, you know.'

Well, I had never been spoken to in my life like this. I immediately thought that I could certainly take advantage of this situation. I stood up, took my belt off and handed it to the auxiliary saying, 'Come on, let's get it over with.'

'Oh really, Jimmy, what a laddie you are, always joking and kidding,' says the auxiliary.

'What's all this about?' asks Dr Robb.

'Well, sir,' I replied, 'when we run away and are brought back we're given a hammering and a cold bath and a glass of Crutin Oil.'

End result: lots of embarrassment all round.

But my satisfaction was short-lived. One of the nurses came in the next morning and said, 'Don't think you're bloody well getting away with that, sonny. You're not.'

I knew it had to come whether it be the next day or a few days later. Eventually it did. I was hammered, bathed and given the Crutin Oil. Another few days' sitting on the toilet pan followed. But I did think that maybe I had given the doctor some food for thought and it was good to see the auxiliary being caught on the hop. These little things were to keep me going in places like Baldovan because if you gave up and sat and vegetated you would just slip into the world they wanted to keep you in.

Life was difficult in those days but I approached each day with anticipation that something good would come out of it. It rarely did but I felt it kept me going. If you want to keep your sanity and give yourself a reason for going on you have to keep thinking that something good will eventually happen. I would also do a lot of thinking. As you had a fair bit of time on your hands, and as I have said before everyone wants to be of good report, you'd almost have a dress rehearsal about what you might say to a nurse and how he or she might reply. Although this may sound a bit strange to some it was a way of keeping the mind active. But it does add to the traumas the mind goes through and I suppose it would have been easier on myself to have given up. But I loved life too much to just give up. Despite all the incidents which happened I still loved life. Sometimes I'd look forward years and think how great it would be to be in my own house, have a job, buy my own clothes – things that 'normal' people take for granted.

But what really kept me going was *me*. I lived life to the full as far as we were allowed. Going out on the farms was hard work but you were out there away from the institution, talking to the old ploughmen in their bothy. These were happenings, good happenings. At night, you'd sit and talk in the dormitory about what Geordie the ploughman had said and what he had told you. To anyone else these things sound unimportant; to me they were my life blood.

But life is lonely when you're trying to retain what sanity you have left and this, in institutions such as Baldovan, led you to participate in whatever area you felt would add to your popularity and maybe make living there more bearable. In institutions such as Baldovan homosexuality among the boys was rife. I had my first experience when I was twelve or thirteen. At first it wasn't the complete homosexual act. That came later. One night a boy of about sixteen crept into my bed beside me. He began kissing my neck and fondling me. It was very frightening at first but, in truth, I began to accept it and waited in anticipation for it. You also learned that this older boy would be your protector and that was great. You had a guardian to look after you in times of need. Wrong though it was – circumstances being what they were – it was necessity more than need. I must say that until it happened I didn't realize it was so common in the institution. Mental defectives are very secretive. I did tell one lad from Aberdeen, with whom I was friendly, after my first experience. He told me that it was going on all the time but not to tell anyone else.

Having a protector brought all sorts of rewards. If I was on punishment he'd bring me extra bread at night and steal milk for me. He'd give me cigarettes. You wanted for nothing. He'd give you part of his ration of sweets when they were issued at the end of the month. At bath time he'd bathe you, that was part of the deal and while the staff were there they turned a blind eye to anything that was going on at bathing time. While there was a lot of homosexuality amongst the boys, and the staff tolerated it, very few of the staff got involved in it. There was one nurse – a retired sailor – who had one boy as his plaything but then again he was good to him and was good to us all by handing out cigarettes and sweets. While I am not proud of this time in my life and later, when my homosexuality would lead me to further problems,

I must repeat that, considering the situation at that time, I believe that I'm entitled to call myself only a 'circumstantial homosexual'.

Today I still bear the mental scars from Baldovan and the physical scars as well. While in Pavilion 5, one Saturday morning I had been cheeky to Madame Plump so I was sent to bed. My friend Johnny came up to the dormitory and told me that my parcel from my mother had arrived and was in the general locker which was unlocked. While everyone else was in the dining hall I sneaked downstairs and got my parcel. Just at the turn of the stairs another nurse came out of the dining room and caught me. He immediately reported me to Madame Plump. I raced upstairs and hid my parcel under someone else's bed at the top of the dormitory and ran back to my bed which was in the middle of the room. Then in comes Madame Plump, marching down the dormitory with a belt in her hand. 'Oh Christ,' I said. 'No more. I'm not taking this any more.' I got up and smashed my hands through the window, slashing my wrists. Madame Plump screamed and panicked. Not being a real nurse she didn't know what to do. Fortunately by then at Baldovan we had one or two trained nurses, one of whom, Sister Rose, was called to the dormitory. She came rushing in and I remember she gave me two particular tablets to swallow. Probably something to calm me down. They couldn't stop the bleeding so I was rushed to Dundee Royal Infirmary and immediately taken into the operating theatre. When I came round in the recovery room who should be sitting at the bedside but Madame Plump? What a way to waken up after an operation. The surgeon came in to see me and said that I was a very lucky lad. I had missed the main artery by about an eighth of an inch. He said that he thought I should stay in the hospital for a few days but Madame Plump said that they were taking me back to the institution.

That, in many ways, was the start of a period of decline in my life. I began to let them know that they weren't getting away with it any longer. So their only get-out was paraldehyde, a sedative, the old asylum stand-by. It's the most safe drug as a sedative but after you took it you stank to high heaven. Paraldehyde comes in two versions – clear and emulsified. Either way it racks your throat as you put it down and it really knocks you out. I was given my dosage every night at eight o'clock. One night when I just couldn't bear the smell from my own body any more I threw the dosage at the night nurse saying, 'If I smell like this why shouldn't you!' She turned to me and said, 'I'm going to get another glass of paraldehyde for you. Will I get outside assistance or will you take it?' I knew that there was no sense resisting. It was better to take it yourself than have it forced down your throat. I then went through a very subdued period of my life. I had lost much of the power of my right arm following the window-smashing incident but while I was aware of what was going on around me I didn't put any guts into doing anything about it. The paraldehyde certainly worked.

37

By then my mother had stopped visiting. She had gone to live in Glasgow. She still wrote and sent parcels, but ceased coming to see me.

I have never blamed her for sending me away and by the time she stopped visiting me I was getting older and beginning to cope with life in the institution. My life was full despite the rights and wrongs of the institution. I never gave the lack of visits any serious thought because we were still in contact by letter. I don't know what would have happened if the letters had stopped, but they never did. Her letters were always full of news. George getting a new job, how Granny was and what Uncle John had told her. My replies were far less exciting. All I could tell her was that I was working on the farm, it was nice weather and we had cheese sandwiches. Hardly the stuff that riveting letters are made of, but she was always glad to hear from me. But this was all part of the façade. I think it should be understood at this point that I had become steeped in the system. You don't necessarily like it and you try to dip in and out of it. You try to live with it but not accept it. In other words you tolerate it. Toleration and acceptance are two totally different things. As time goes on, as has happened to me, and I'm sure has happened to others, you learn to hold on to your ideals, your principles. You never lose them. You tuck them away in your back pocket and they are there for ever. But you know there's no room for them in an institution. How in hell am I going to go downstairs and say to a nurse that it's a pleasant day today and I would like to go to the golf course? No, what you did was you wondered what was going on in the laundry today. Is so and so off today and things like that. You play along with the system when it suits you.

Baldovan was typical of the system. It was a refined Oliver Twist existence. It was a dumping ground for unmanageable children, with all sorts there from working-class lads and lassies to those of the rich who couldn't cope with them at home. Sadly, it was invariably the children of the richer people who didn't receive visitors. You existed from day to day. You were all grouped together. There were no individuals, you were a collective. Everyone was to have a Paris bun, without exception. Everybody would be put to bed at seven-thirty. You weren't allowed to be an individual. You were one of the crew, you sailed in the same ship obeying the same rules. There were some happy moments but you made those yourself. There were some good, loving, caring nurses but they were in the minority. Where you have an authoritative regime where someone wants to rule with the whip, the good ones can do only so much. Even they can't change the system. The attitude from those in charge is 'Who the hell do you think you are, nurse? Coming in here and paying attention to them. The next thing you'll be doing is kissing them goodnight.'

I believe that it could have been different if the nursing staff had been trained properly and taught to understand the children rather than make them do what the system required of them. If we had had more nurses like Sister Rose rather than Madame Plump, if the doctors had been more like Dr Robb there would certainly have been an improvement in the quality of life. Would it have been so bad to have met up with the girls at Baldovan more than once a year at Christmas time? Many a lad fell in love from a distance. Even at the Christmas Dance there was to be no close dancing. But the main problem was that there was no redress. That didn't happen in mental institutions until the late Sixties. At Baldovan during that period you got your hammering right in front of people. The authorities had no fear because they knew there was nothing you could do about it. If anyone did sustain an injury such as a black eye or a burst lip after having been slapped about the head, no-one bothered to investigate what happened. After all, if you're a mental defective it's always self-inflicted.

3

Murthly

I had been at Baldovan for almost nine years when one day, right out of the blue, I was told by a nurse that I was to get dressed and that I was going to a new hospital. No reason was given and when I persisted with my questioning I was told the usual reason. 'It'll be good for you.'

I was taken along to the doctor's office where I was introduced to another doctor and also someone else, an old man who, to look at, seemed more in need of treatment than myself. We left Baldovan in a Rolls-Royce belonging to the Council. As we got into the car the new doctor handed me ten Woodbines. How unfitting, smoking Woodbines in the back of a Rolls-Royce! We travelled from Dundee to Perth not by the main roads but by back roads and eventually arrived at Murthly, just outside Perth. I was received by a big hefty attendant. This was the first time I had been in an asylum. It hit me like a ton of bricks. On the way down the corridor you could hear the other patients saying,

'Oh, a new patient, a new patient.' I ended up in the admission ward at the south end of the asylum. In mental institutions the procedure never changed for admissions. All clothes off, a bath and into bed. I hadn't cried in a long time but, oh, how I cried that day. I was the only adolescent in the ward. All around me were poor-looking, old men, lying constantly in bed twenty-four hours a day. At about six o'clock that evening Dr McDougal, the head of the asylum and a psychiatrist, arrived in the ward. 'Och, look at that poor laddie. Let him up.' I got up and was taken to a store and issued with what we called the parish tweeds. Your own possessions were put away in mothballs for the time when you got out, if ever. The suit was grey in colour and I was issued with long army underpants, an army vest, socks and a pair of heavy shoes.

I was then sent to my new ward. There were twenty beds in the ward. Down the middle was a strip of linoleum which was polished every day along with the floor. There was a small table in the middle of the ward and a couple of *chaises-longues*. There were curtains but everything had that standard institutional look about it. In the ward, I realized, were some who had come from the war and some who had been in for a long time. As I was the latest recruit, I was put in the admission bed which was in the centre of the ward where you could be observed at all times. There was one old man in the bed beside mine. I have never seen a person in such a state, and was really upset. I learned later that his cough was simply the death rattle. He soon died. Another patient was a former bank manager from Perth, who always had plenty of money. If you did something for him he would give you a shilling. Another was a soldier, who would suddenly crouch down behind the sofa and start pretending to shoot at something which he saw in his mind. But instead of trying to placate him the nurses would consider him a nuisance and say, 'For Christ's sake, get him into the room out the bloody way.' The nursing standard at Murthly was, sadly, no different from Baldovan. Get them up, feed them, make sure they don't cause any trouble – that was the working code. Very quickly, as I looked around, I realized that this was a very different place from Baldovan. Looking at the other patients' faces you could see the different stories: aggressive, depressive, oppressive.

At the north end of the building there was a small ward of eight people who were considered to be 'very disturbed'. There was one lad who came from Dundee. He had been at West Green Hospital (now known as the Royal Liff Hospital). His mother had had him transferred from West Green because of his treatment there. At night these patients, like ourselves, went upstairs to bed: we at one end of the building, they at the other. The routine was that the night nurse – I use the term loosely – would come on duty, get the hand-over from his day counterpart, then settle himself down on a couch with a blanket round him and go off to sleep. Well you never dared disturb the night nurse, but the lad from Dundee did. He shook the nurse to waken him saying, 'You're not supposed to be doing that. You're supposed to be looking after us.' The nurse, together with another from the next ward, turned on him and started to kick the living nightlights out of him. This was the first of many such beatings I was to witness in the years to come. Fortunately, one of the nurses, Geordie, was a bit better than the other. I said, 'For God's sake, stop it. You'll kill him.' The other nurse told me to 'Fuck off' or I would get the same but I said to Geordie, 'Come on, that's no' like you, you'll kill him.' His face turned white as a sheet. He now knew that should anything happen there was a witness. They stopped beating the lad from Dundee. My cold baths and hammerings at Baldovan were nothing compared to this. And this happened when I had been in the place less than two weeks.

Later that week I was sitting on a bench beside the cricket pitch when a senior member of staff came along. I asked why two or three nurses would want to beat up a patient. Without answering he got up and walked away. He didn't want any trouble.

The daily routine at Murthly was slightly different from Baldovan although there were many similarities. Fortunately incontinence was tolerated. This was because of the ages of most of them and you can hardly go around hammering old men, just because they were incontinent, in front of everyone. In the morning they were the first to be got up, usually around five-thirty. Some of them were incontinent even out of bed and they were dressed in white moleskins. It is bad enough to be incontinent but to be picked out like that was a disgrace. They were made to stand in a line down the wards until everyone else was ready. No question of their being allowed to sit down and wait. We all made our own beds, not in the hospital style but in the army style with the blankets folded perfectly and the pillow cases pointing in the right direction. We also had to make sure that the castors on our beds were all facing the right way. There was actually more attention paid to this than to the nursing. We would then all troop downstairs to the washroom where the geriatric mental patients would have their faces washed and their hair combed. There was a terrible vacant look in these old people's faces. You felt that the day they met their maker would be their greatest freedom. But nothing was really being done for them in the true nursing sense. I started taking it on myself to make their beds in the ward. I also ended up washing the shitty sheets in the laundry area. For this task I got an extra ten cigarettes a week. But the greatest satisfaction I got was when I'd wash and change some old man's clothes and sheets where he had been lying in his own urine for hours. The nurse never bothered with the regulation time for checking. To see his face after I had finished with him; if he could have said thanks he would have – his expression said enough. As to the reasons behind my getting involved in all of this, it was all part of once again making sure that I was of good report. One day Dr McDougal came round; he knew I was doing these things, and said, 'Why don't you get into this game yourself, Jimmy?'

We all had our meals together, thirty to a table. No disrespect to the old folk but I made it my business to be at the top end of the table where the serving started. The porridge was served from the top end and passed down the table and it isn't a pretty sight to have someone whose nose is running and is spluttering and slavering doing it over your porridge as it is passed to you.

But they weren't all like that. There was a rich variety of souls there. We had a Captain from the war who came from Crieff. Although very disturbed at times he was a thorough gentleman. He was allowed to wear his own clothes and he would march up and down all day. That's what the war had done to him. There were others who seemed pretty sensible and you could have quite a conversation with them. I remember one, in particular, who came from Aberfeldy. He, luckily, was allowed out not long after I arrived.

Unlike Baldovan, where there was therapy of sorts, there was nothing at Murthly. Apart from keeping on the right side of the authorities my bed-making and washing the soiled linen kept me active. It also had its benefits. Apart from the extra cigarettes I was also given tea and toast in the mornings around ten o'clock. That was real favouritism!

There was only one working party; the less fortunate would sit around all day in the sitting room. The head attendant would come in with the bogey roll tobacco round his arms like a rope and twist off enough to fill their pipes and they would sit there

all day puffing away. They never asked for anything and never got anything. One of the few good
things that happened at Murthly was that if parents
wanted their child *out* of there Dr McDougal never
stood in their way. In the outside world there was
a slightly increasing awareness then of mental illness by some parents and they would come for
their child. One chap, who was about twenty-four
and had been there for six years, was let out and
the next I heard of him was that he was married and had five children. Thank God his parents
realized they could get him out.

The nursing staff at Murthly, like Baldovan, were
not 'nurses' in the true sense of the word. While
the majority wouldn't really bother you, there
was a rotten minority. But it was a powerful
minority. Even the good ones would never bear
witness against the bad ones. One of the really
sadistic nurses used to enjoy punching patients in
the stomach. He took great delight in doing it. If
any of the older patients got out of bed or untidied
their beds he'd scream at them, 'Lie down and
go to bloody sleep.' This went on all day and
he didn't want to be disturbed. If the screaming
failed he would then punch them repeatedly in the
stomach to make them stay in bed.

Of the good ones there was an old chap whom
we called Trochry — he came from the village
of Trochry in Perthshire. He understood the old
men. He would laugh with them and cry with
them. You have to know when to say, 'That's
enough,' when to laugh and when to cajole. That

all comes from understanding human beings and particularly the mental defective.

At Murthly I learned to study the moods of people, not only the patients but also the staff. I still wasn't confident enough to play the kind of games or stunts you could pull at Baldovan and get away with it. But I was learning all the time. You get to know your guardians, their moods, the way they perform. It's all part of the survival plan. If I learn that a nurse is going to react badly to something I may say or do then I don't. I learn what he likes, what he dislikes. He may be in a pig of a mood some days but you learn what to say to take him out of it. It could be something really simple such as, 'I saw your wife down in the village there. Oh, you're a lucky man to have such a lovely wife,' and then everything would change for the better, and some poor soul on whom he was going to take out his temper would get away. It's all part of the game you play and the longer I was there the more I learned. You would have a dress-rehearsal of what you wanted to do. If, say, I wanted something on the tenth of April I started preparing for it well in advance. You would watch and listen, then, at the right time, you'd begin to place it into the charge nurse's, or whoever's, mind and by the tenth you got what you wanted. All this effort for what usually turned out to be a very minor request.

My mother did come to visit me once at Murthly. We had still been writing but less frequently. I think that because it was an asylum that I was in now she was a bit frightened of the place. After a visit the nurses always spoke to the visitor, particularly if it was a patient's relative. You never got to hear what they were saying but no doubt it was the usual. 'Oh yes, Jimmy's doing very well here. It's doing him the world of good.'

Eventually after I had been there for a while I was allowed down to the little confectioner's shop in the village and then eventually allowed into Perth. I was very keen on the theatre and at Murthly they let you put on little plays sometimes. So it was a great delight to go and see the real thing in Perth. The theatre always sent up complimentary tickets and I always made sure that I got one. I liked period plays such as *Gaslight*, *Journey's End* and *Hasty Heart*. I once saw Valerie Lush in *Dracula*. These nights out made life a little more tolerable, but even so I still longed for my freedom. I began to abscond.

I made my way to Glasgow by hitching lifts on lorries and arrived at the North British Hotel in George Square where my brother Billy worked. 'Oh God, what are you doing here?' was the welcome I got from Billy. But he'd give me a few shillings for something to eat and I'd move on. At this time my mother had set up house with Jock McNab, with whom she had gone off to work in Cornwall for the summer season. I went up to her house and, of course, McNab was there. 'You'll have to go back, you know,' he would say, but my mother would let me stay the night, give me a meal and then I'd go back in the morning. Unfortunately the time was never right to talk to my mother. McNab was always there and I never got the chance to talk to her on my own. At this stage I must say that it didn't really bother me that my mother didn't make any effort to get me away from Murthly. I had been a year and a half in Murthly, and although there were many things I certainly didn't approve of at Murthly, I had carved out my own niche there. I was able to get on and off a bus, walk down the High Street in Perth never looking out of place. I enjoyed it to a degree because in many ways I was nursing. I was looking after my own, trying to improve their life. In the outside world anyone can look unhappy but invariably they get over it quickly. In a mental asylum it's more difficult. There are so many diversions and avenues that the mental patient ends up in on his way back to happiness. Knowing this I was able to bring them through with a laugh and a joke and even sometimes a tear. Sometimes it would be something very simple like starting a game of cards and then admitting to cheating which would get them laughing. One thing that helped at Murthly was the number of visits which were available. Wednesdays, Saturdays and Sundays every week. But sadly, like Baldovan, there were many who didn't get a visitor and some took it hard.

Murthly was a good example of the different kinds of mental patients that you got under one roof. They weren't completely mental, certainly not in the criminal sense; I would describe them as more of a nuisance value. Some certainly would sit around and vegetate but others would become self-deluded and create their own characters. There weren't many but I've seen a number who each claimed to be Jesus Christ and we had Popes and Kings. Now I see no harm in someone in their fifties, sixties or seventies thinking themselves to be the British Monarch or President of the United States. Not at their stage of life stuck in an asylum. When these people thought themselves King or Queen they were happy. We learned to live with it saying, 'Good morning, Your Highness', and there was no harm in that. Maybe that isn't insanity. Maybe it's a choice in life. Who are we to say it's wrong when someone at a particular stage in their life, who is in an asylum, says, 'To hell with it. I'm here and I'm going to enjoy myself. I'm going to create a position for myself here'? No-one questions this properly when someone says, 'To hell with it, I'm going to be the Provost of Perth.' How we sit back and, with a shake of the head, say, 'Delusions of grandeur, madness.' It's maybe a cool, calculated course of action they have taken to get away from the humdrum life they are leading. But what was the reaction of the authorities? They would come along and give them tranquillizers. After that they sat, day after day. Their lives, their kingdoms, their mansions were no more. Now that to me is cruel. A psychiatrist will tell a visiting member of the family, 'Oh yes, John thinks he's a king and we've had to put him on tranquillizers for his own good.' But did anyone ever try to talk to John about it and if he was happy then why not let him be? Tranquillizers are the ruination of man but also, as far as the system is concerned, the easy way out. At Murthly they used a variety of tablets and medicines such as Phenobarbitone and, for epileptic patients, Epineuton. And, of course, there was the old favourite, bromide. Bromide we used a lot at that time. You could always tell those who used it – they came out in spots. At night when the night nurse would come on there would be a large Winchester bottle full of bromide. By morning it had all gone and no-one asked any questions. It seems quite amazing looking back, that here we were in the late Forties and early Fifties, and there was still no real progress in the way that mental patients were treated for their illness. It was still just a case of admitting a patient to an institution and as long as he or she was quite well behaved there would be no trouble. The authorities simply wanted to get through the day without any hassle.

From the patient's point of view one of the pleasant things at Murthly was the contact you had with the female patients. You were allowed to walk down to the shop with them and in latter years some of the patients got married to each other. In my case, though, my attention was being diverted by a young nurse who worked in the women's section. I had passed her a few times during my tasks and then I found out that she fancied me. God knows why! I didn't have a clue what to do, never having experienced any real contact with women. She arranged that we would go to Perth to the theatre. On the way home we got off the bus before Murthly and began to walk.

It was a beautiful summer evening. We sat down at the side of a burn and talked. Later she began to kiss me and fondle me. She did everything to arouse me but I could not perform.

After her departure I continued to abscond as often as I could. Unlike Baldovan, where you got the 'treatment', when you returned the only thing you lost was your parole privileges. You soon learned that after a suitable time you could ask for ground parole and then later outside parole.

By now at Murthly I had graduated to having my own room. It was a great relief. The early days I found degrading. The asylum was packed full after the war and where there were supposed to be, say, twelve beds there would be twenty. You could not walk straight up to your bed, you had to slide up between two other beds. And by then I was able to have my own towel and soap which I had managed to acquire.

When I was transferred from Baldovan to Murthly I was never given any reason and the same was the case when, one day, I was told that I was going away to my sister's house in Orkney. I went to bed as usual at seven-thirty but was awakened again at eleven o'clock. I was taken to the station in the doctor's car and my ticket was bought from Perth to Thurso. I never asked any questions because you didn't ask questions when you were in an asylum. You followed orders. I felt very happy about it although I did feel I should have a suitcase, some money in my pocket and my papers. I had nothing like that. I was given ten shillings by the doctor but that wasn't for me to spend, it was for my ferry fare from the mainland to Orkney. I got on at Scrabster and sailed for Stromness where my sister met me.

On the train I did a lot of thinking. Obviously it had all been planned. There must have been letters and other correspondence but why wasn't I told? At the end of the day I found out that it was my dear mother who had engineered all of this to see how I would get on, but it proved a fatal mistake.

My sister didn't say very much to me. Although I was happy to be away from Murthly it certainly wasn't the life I wanted. I was expected to help with the harvest and immediately I thought back to the cheap labour scheme that was operated at Baldovan. I stayed there for about six weeks but I couldn't stand the life nor could I sleep in the straw bed at the croft. I wanted to better myself in this life. In the mornings you washed in a barrel of cold water outside the croft and then spent all day at the threshing. However that wasn't why I left. I had been made quite welcome but I was more like a package being mailed from one place to another. I wasn't prepared to accept that. We had good food. We never bought bread, huge scones were made on the range in the kitchen. But one day I asked my sister if I could have some money to spend while I was in Kirkwall. You'd have thought I was asking for the moon. Words were exchanged and I said, 'I've been working at the threshing and cleaning the house for the past six weeks without a break.' She replied, 'Considering you're not one of us, you're damned lucky to be here.' This cut me to the quick. To explain, my middle name is McLaughlin and that was the same name as the family who lived down the road from us in Perth. My father had been friendly with the family and I always had a suspicion that I was the child of Mrs McLaughlin and that my mother had taken me in. In short, I was a bastard. In the past I had remembered comments from both my mother and my father and sometimes from my brothers and sisters that I was not really part of their family. I told my sister that I was leaving. She gave me some money for my fare and I headed for Perth where I got in contact with my brother George. He confirmed my suspicions when I told him the story. When I questioned him more he said, well, yes, it was as I had thought.

I was glad to be away from Orkney. I felt I was being used there. Being an asylum patient is something that takes a long time to shake off. On the journey back to Perth I did a lot of thinking and came to the conclusion that if I was my father's 'mistake' then maybe that's why he didn't really love me. Every time he saw me he was reminded of his 'mistake'.

I arrived back at Murthly of my own volition at about eleven o'clock. I went to the home of the doctor. He came to the door with his velvet smoking jacket on. 'What are you doing here?'

'I've come back,' I said.

He took me over to the head attendant and told him to give me a bed. And that was it. Nobody bothered about me. It was as if I had never been away. No-one came to me and asked what had happened, why I had left or anything like that. It was typical of the regime. It was just a case of 'Jimmy's back. Now let's get back to normal.'

Despite the fact that at Murthly they were dealing with the mentally ill, not mental defectives, there was no-one there to try to cure them. We had everything there from senile dementia through to the psychotic. There's a decided difference between the insane person and the mentally deficient. The only continuity or sameness was the type of treatment. They all had the same approach. Let's get it over and done with and get back to a quiet life. There were no plans, no psychoanalysis, as there is today. The only psychoanalysts in those days were in Harley Street, London. Certainly not at Murthly Hospital, near Perth. But the patients knew within themselves; they didn't have to tell you. You could sense it, see it in their faces, they were just there, in the asylum, lost to the world. The hardest to take was the treatment meted out to the very disturbed patients. Fear doesn't enter into it as far as the patient is concerned. If you're in such a state as the severely disturbed, fear is the last thing on your mind. The treatment had been the same since the days of Bedlam. The authorities' answer was to beat the badness out of them. Although they would quieten a patient down he was being cowed and then he would learn fear. Quieten him down by whatever means and then we'll get back to a quiet life. That was the pivotal thinking of the system.

4

Out of the Frying Pan Into the Fire

I had returned from my escapade in Orkney in the early Fifties and now in the mid-Fifties I began to plan what I hoped would be my final escape to freedom. I was going to take advantage of the McNaghten Rules which were in force in those days. These rules stated that if a mental patient or mental defective was able to remain at large for a suitable period by fending for himself then he would be considered able to look after himself and would be a free man.

It took about three or four weeks to plan and prepare for my departure. Rather than the usual way of absconding by jumping on a bus I worked out that I needed respectable-looking clothes and shoes, a good coat and some money. I began offering to clean out the nurses' room and they gave me their empty beer bottles which I exchanged for money. I got clothes from other patients who had some to spare. As I told them, say, that I had torn my underwear, they never questioned my requests.

I also amassed quite a collection of items such as sewing materials, razor, shaving brush and soap. I knew that if I made it to Glasgow, which was my intended destination, I would need to look presentable if I was to find a job. Fortunately I still had my own room at Murthly and as I was a tidy person, together with the fact that the nurses couldn't give a damn about you, that meant that no-one ever came to check the room so I managed to hide everything in my locker. The one major problem I had to overcome was to ensure that the double doors to the outside from our building were unlocked. They were left open during the day but at night the outer door of the two was always locked. I needed to get a routine going that would allow me access to the key so I began helping the nurse, old Trochry, to lock up at night. 'Give me your key and I'll lock up for you, Trochry,' I'd say. 'Aye, OK, but mind you do it properly or I'll get into trouble,' he'd reply. Night upon night we carried on this routine until the night I decided to go. When it came to locking-up time I had placed my suitcase outside the door while pretending to lock up. I knew that the bus into Perth would be passing at about seven-fifteen. If I missed that the plan failed. When Trochry went back into his room I made my move. There were other patients around the door at the time but none of them bothered to even ask where I was going. Once out of the door I cut through the gardens and made for the back gate. It was screened from the building by trees unlike the front gate where I could have been seen. The adrenalin was pumping through my veins and I was breathing heavily as I arrived at the bus stop. Waiting those two minutes for the bus to arrive seemed like eternity. I kept looking over my shoulder in case anyone was following and thinking all the time whether there'd be anyone on the bus who might recognize me. The bus arrived, a double-decker with the open platform to the rear. I got on, shoved my case into the luggage space and went upstairs. During the short journey to Perth my stomach churned so much at one stage I thought I was going to be sick.

I reached Perth about eight o'clock. It's a very different city today. Then there was a vast number of alleyways and little back streets. I knew them all. I made my way to the old transport café on the Edinburgh Road. It's a car park now, but at that time there was a transport café which had been converted out of an old theatre. By luck there was a lorry going to Glasgow and it gave me the lift I required. I don't remember saying much to the driver. I actually slept most of the way as I was so exhausted from the trauma of my escape. We arrived in Glasgow at about half past ten and I set off for the Great Eastern or, as we used to call it, the Duke Street Hotel. I had over three pounds in my pocket and when you consider that a bed for the night in those days was only one shilling and sixpence I was rich! I booked in for just one night. The next day I spent my time trying to orientate myself. I could have rushed in to try and find a job but I decided to take stock of things first. I thought that I might get a job in Lewis's or as a hotel porter, like my brother Billy at the North British. He might be able to help. That evening I ended up at the coffee stall in St Vincent Street. I stood around watching what was going on. Two policemen walked by and said to me, 'Come on, darling, move along.' I think they thought I was importuning. Well, I didn't want any dealings with the police at this stage so I moved on. I felt rather angry at them. It had never crossed my mind that people would hang around coffee bars to pick up homosexuals. As far as I was concerned my only contact with homosexuality had been in institutions. I wandered about watching the comings and goings of the prostitutes in the area. Taxis would draw up, the girls would get in, then later a girl would arrive back at the coffee stall, business completed.

As I was there this young man, in his mid-twenties I would say, came up to me and began to chat. He offered to buy me a hot dog and a coffee which I accepted. How gullible I was. He asked me if I needed a bed for the night. I was delighted to accept. As far as I was concerned, having spent over fifteen years in institutions where there was rarely a friendly face, I was delighted to go along with his offer. It seemed so kind. And I did think that it would save me some money. We left the coffee stall and walked to a house not far from St Vincent Street. I don't remember the exact address but I recall passing the post office in George Square. We went into a close and up the stairs. He opened the door, there was no-one in the house. He made a cup of tea and we chatted about jobs. He said that there were plenty of jobs in Glasgow and that I would have no trouble in finding one. Eventually we went to bed. There was only one bed in the room, in the recess of the kitchen living room. I had no pyjamas so I kept my underwear on. During the night I was awakened by him kissing me and fondling me. I was rigid with fear. What on earth had I got myself into? He continued, and I let him bugger me. I know it would be easy to think that I could have stopped him or I could have got up and run away, but fear does terrible things to you. Afterwards I went back to sleep.

I was awoken in the morning by a hand shaking me. Standing at the end of the bed was a man and woman. 'What the fucking hell's going on here?' inquired the man. I said, 'There was a chappie.' Before I could explain further the man turned to the woman, exclaiming 'That dirty bastard', adding 'Get up and get out.' As I got up I saw to my horror that every stitch I had was gone. My 'friend' had stolen everything including my suitcase. Fortunately the woman took pity on me. I think that the couple must have known who the other man was; maybe a relation and they didn't want any trouble. She gave me an old boiler-suit and a pair of wellingtons, two sizes too big; I felt abused and degraded. All my carefully made plans were now in ruins. How was I going to survive with no money and no clothes in which I could apply for a job? I left the house and made for George Square where I just sat and thought. I felt filthy and I thought that everyone must be looking at me. For someone like myself who has always taken pride in his appearance to now be clothed in a dirty old boiler-suit and oversized wellingtons was very difficult to take. Through my mind time and time again that day came the experience of the previous night. Homosexuality in the outside world? Never. That sort of thing only happens inside in places like Baldovan.

With great trepidation I made my way back to the Great Eastern where I explained my predicament to the man on the desk. He said that he knew someone who would help me. I went and sat in the lounge until teatime when they gave me something to eat. About six o'clock my name was called out and I went to the front desk where there was a chap and his wife. They took me to their house and fitted me out with clothes. They were very Christian people although they didn't mention religion to me but they did talk about the perils of wandering about big cities when I told them what had happened to me. The chap was the same size as me and he gave me a lovely pin-striped suit. They also gave me three pounds and finally saw me on to the bus back into the city-centre and the Great Eastern. Thank God for those two lovely people. At that stage I was really feeling down and while they couldn't do much for my inner self they gave the outer man back his respectability.

In some ways that whole incident showed me how naive I was. While I was confident that I could make my way in the outside world I hadn't taken into consideration just how devious the outside world could be. Mental patients fall into a few recognizable categories. In the outside world I found to my cost that there are very many more unrecognizable categories. My confidence had certainly taken a knock but I was determined to see out the twenty-eight days under the McNaghten Rules.

I went to the old standby, my brother Billy, who was still at the hotel. As in the past his first greeting was, 'What the hell are you up to now?' I couldn't tell him the story of what had happened. If I had told him one part of the story, that a chap had offered me a bed for the night and then stolen my clothes, I would have had to unfold the rest of the story. Billy had been living in Glasgow long enough to be able to put two and two together. 'Your mum's going to be awful upset if she finds out that you've run away again,' said Billy. 'I'll be all right,' I replied. I don't know what I wanted from Billy. I think probably a little understanding. I was feeling very low. To say it was due to any mental condition would be wrong. When people are robbed they feel that their private lives have been invaded. That was how I felt then. This and all the other emotions were churning through my head. I also wanted to go and see my mother but I felt that I must be careful not to hurt her, she had had enough disappointments in her life and by now no doubt my sister in Orkney would have written to her telling her how much of a disaster I had been and that I had upped and left and gone back to the asylum.

I spent the day after seeing Billy wandering around Glasgow looking in shop windows trying to pluck up the courage to go to my mother's house.

I knew she wouldn't turn me away from the door but she would feel that she should send me back to Murthly. I think that the way ahead would have been a bit easier for me if I hadn't had the set-back. Before going up to her house I wandered around Cathedral Street, Rotten Row and streets such as MacAuslin Street and Taylor Street, and places that no longer exist today. Eventually, with bated breath I went up to her house. When she opened the door she said, 'Oh, my God, what are you doing here?'

'I'm home,' I said. Then McNab, whom she was still living with, appeared and said, 'You cannae do that.'

I thought, 'I hate you, you bastard.' I began crying and Mother began crying too. McNab's answer to all of this was, 'Here's some money for you to keep you going.' This was no answer. What I wanted to do was to sit and talk to my mother, just the two of us. Yes, I wanted to stay with her but, as it was only one room with a scullery off it, that would have been impractical. But what cruelty from McNab. Didn't he realize that my mother may also have wanted me to stay or at least be near her? Before leaving I told my mother that I had a bed at the Great Eastern and that seemed to cheer her up but her face fell when McNab told me not to be coming around bothering her all the time.

When I left her house my emotions were in a turmoil. McNab had upset me very much, but more so he had upset my mother and that was unforgivable in my mind. The whole incident had wrenched me, twisted me, to such an extent that I really was a mental wreck. I'll never know what possessed me to do what I did next. All I wanted to do was lay my head down and sleep. I was being so tormented by my thoughts. I went up to a policeman in the street and said, 'I'm going to kill Jock McNab.' As soon as I said it I thought, 'My God, what have I done?' But by then it was too late. Immediately, I regretted having said it and had cause to regret it for many years thereafter. The policeman took me to the local police station in Cowcaddens where I was charged with breach of the peace.

There are those who would say that this outburst was because I was mentally unstable. I can't agree with that. I was upset by all that had gone on over the past few days and more particularly by what had happened at my mother's house. How many people in normal households have a fight and the husband screams, 'I'm going to kill you one of these days, my lady!' Or two chaps who dislike each other meet on the street and one says, 'I'm going to get you, boy!' Are these examples of mental instability? Just because you come from an asylum doesn't necessarily mean that all your actions and words can be attributed to mental illness.

Once inside the police station I gave them my mother's address and then later on sandwiches and cigarettes arrived for me. I think that Billy brought them down. The police contacted my mother who told them all about me and where I had come from. I appeared in open court and was formally charged with breach of the peace by the Procurator-Fiscal. I was detained for medical reports. Standing in the dock I had, at first, great apprehension about being sent to prison. But I did think that maybe if I got thirty days or so that would be the end of it and thirty days in prison would be better than being sent back to Murthly.

A group of us who had appeared on that day were taken in a Black Maria to Barlinnie. On the way there one of the men told me that I had nothing to worry about; that he was in for much more and would soon be out on bail. On arrival at Barlinnie I was confronted with a series of commands from the receiving officer. 'Right you. Forward. In there. Strip.' You were stripped and ill-fitting clothing and shoes were literally flung at you. 'Observation,' another shouted and I was taken away to a cell on the ground floor of one of the prison halls with OBS on the door. Apart from half an hour each day when the Observation prisoners were allowed out to exercise together, we were kept in our cells. Meals were brought to the cell and the warders continually checked you through the peep-hole in the door.

It was at Barlinnie that I first came across common talk of religious bigotry. While exercising one day in the yard another prisoner and I got talking and I told him about my case. He asked what religion I was. I replied that I didn't really have any religion. He told me to say that I was a Protestant if I was asked by them. 'They hate Catholics,' he told me. 'If you say you're a Protestant you'll be sent to a mental hospital. If you say you're a Catholic they'll send you straight to the Criminal Lunatic Department in Perth. That's how much they hate

Catholics.' Later, when asked my religion, I was nearly tempted to say Catholic to see what would happen but good sense got the better of me.

A few days later two doctors from Gartloch came to see me to interview me. The questions were inane. 'Do you hear voices? Do you feel that people are against you? Do you hate yourself? Do you hate your mother?' It was always to do with hatred. They also asked me, eventually, why I wanted to kill Jock McNab. I told them that I thought that he wasn't the right person for my mother. I don't think that was the answer they wanted as they didn't seem very impressed with it. It was probably too logical for them to understand. After being in Barlinnie for about two weeks I re-appeared in court. I had a 'poor man's lawyer', as he was so called. He just kept saying to me, 'You'll be all right, you'll be all right.' In the court he said that I had committed the breach of the peace while under stress. It all seemed to have been decided beforehand between the Procurator-Fiscal and the Sheriff-Substitute. The verdict handed down was that I be placed in Gartloch Mental Hospital under Section 23:2 (b) which meant that should I commit any further offences then the Procurator-Fiscal could recall me to the court.

I was taken back to Barlinnie and that afternoon transferred by ambulance to Gartloch.

5

Gartloch

On the journey from Barlinnie to Gartloch I thought that it would be very easy to blame everyone else other than myself for what had happened since leaving Murthly. I wasn't so much annoyed or upset by what had happened but I was disappointed that what I had planned for myself hadn't borne fruit. So it was back to the beginning again, back to the seedling part in the hope that I would flourish again.

At that time, in the Fifties, Gartloch was seen as a very modern hospital with up-to-date facilities. They certainly had plenty of doctors and the nursing standard was certainly higher than at Baldovan and Murthly. On arrival at the hospital I was greeted by a friendly male nurse who saw that the two prison officers from Barlinnie still had me handcuffed.

'Get those bloody things off his arms! If he's fit to come here he doesn't need those.'

I thought, 'Christ Almighty! This is a good start. What a change from other institutions.'

I was taken from the admission area and as

usual I was given a bath and put to bed in the admission ward. An L-shaped room with twelve beds, it was decorated in a pleasant manner and was very spacious. There were lockers and each patient had his own towel and soap dish. That was really forward thinking on someone's part. What luxury! Within an hour the doctor came to see me: Dr Alan McDougal. We sat and spoke and he asked me about what had brought me to Gartloch. I told him briefly what had happened and his chats continued with me each day over the next ten days.

The daily routine in the admission ward was very different from what I had experienced in the past. We were all given pyjamas and dressing gowns which you wore for the first three days, then you were issued with clothes. Although you were up as usual at six-thirty there wasn't the same frantic regimentation as in other institutions. They actually seemed to be caring for us. I was to find out later that the admission ward was for them to get to know you and that things were not so free-and-easy in the other wards. Next to H7, the admission ward, was H8, which was almost like a hotel with suites of rooms. These were reserved for the better-off patients, company directors and their like. They were waited on hand and foot. Jock Tamson's bairns, like me, had to do with less.

Following breakfast, which was served in the ward, you'd have your session with Dr McDougal. After about the fifth session he told me to come into his suite, sat me down and gave me a cigarette. He'd look up at me now and again but rarely spoke. I had to make the conversation otherwise he'd think that I was just a vegetable. I felt sure he was writing me up at these sessions. At no time, though, during these sessions was I ever given a hint as to how long I would be in Gartloch. From my past experience I knew it wasn't good to ask.

After Dr McDougal had finished with me I was handed over to another doctor who was a psychoanalyst. I didn't really respond to psychoanalysis; perhaps it was because of the questions, which were concerned with digging into your mind, or so they thought. For example they would ask, 'Now, when you were crossing that bridge you did want to throw yourself off, didn't you?' If you wanted the interview over quickly then you'd make up a story of why you wanted to throw yourself off the bridge and what led up to it and they would be pleased. It was a game we were both playing. But again we're back to winners and losers. You thought you were winning but you weren't really. Psychiatrists are just as cunning and foxy as the people they're interviewing. There were other highly amusing questions which whatever answer you gave you'd be the loser. They'd ask you, 'Would you be comfortable talking to the Queen?' and 'If you were talking to the Queen could you take coffee with her without being embarrassed?' And the *pièce de resistance*: 'Do you have any relations in the Royal Family?' If you replied that you could speak to the Queen, have coffee with her and not feel embarrassed then they put you down as having delusions of grandeur. If, on the other hand, you said that you'd be unable to talk to her and be very embarrassed to take coffee with her they put you down as having an inferiority complex. I think if you said you had relations in the Royal Family they'd have written you off right away!

After the ten days in the admission ward I was moved to A ward, a big barn of a place with an old-fashioned fire in the middle and bare seats all around the wall. There the procedure resembled Murthly in many ways. The ward was over-crowded, no lockers, just a large cupboard with shelves, and, like Murthly, the less sane ones had their laces and braces taken away from them at night in case they tried to damage themselves in any way. We had two very good charge nurses, Tony and John. If the leaders are good then the subordinates take a leaf out of their book and things go well.

About six weeks after arriving at Gartloch I absconded for the first time. As in the case at Baldovan it was done on the spur of the moment. I had been mixing with other Glasgow blokes and heard all the snippets of news from the outside. How easy jobs were to get, what was being paid and how easy it was to get good cheap lodgings. So I decided that I could do all that and I did a flit. There are about a dozen different ways of getting out of Gartloch. Back, front, middle, through the trees to name but a few. The only time a head-count was taken was at meal-times. I went after lunch knowing that I wouldn't be missed until after teatime. I went into Glasgow but didn't go near my mother's house this time. I walked about the city and then thought that I was letting the side down. That's the way I was feeling. I returned of my own accord and was taken back into H7. They told me that they were going to put me on to a treatment. 'We're going to help you,' they said. They put me on to a dreaded drug which was later taken off the list – Sulphonal. It was supposed to be the be-all and end-all of drugs for the cure of the mentally ill. They discovered eventually that it wasn't – and at what cost? It was administered in tablet form crushed into water. Two tablets, three times a day. The effects were unbelievable. Within three days I lost the power of my voice, I was speaking as if I was gaga. I couldn't walk, to such an extent that the nurses had to lift me on to a commode if I wanted to go to the toilet. All this time the dreadful thing was that my brain was still functioning normally but I couldn't tell anyone because I couldn't speak. I lay in bed for three months and during that time they brought a speech therapist to teach me how to speak again. Apparently they thought that this was part of getting better. You go in grey at this end, get blacker, then come out white at the other end. They stopped the treatment after three months and, fortunately, they stopped using the drug at all not long after that. While my reaction was bad enough I believe a few patients died from it. While no hospital wants their patients to die from a treatment, the experimental nature of mental health care at that time was such that any deaths would just become a statistic when they came to evaluating the drug later.

Obviously there had been too many problems with Sulphonal and that's why they stopped using it.

Once I came off the tablets it took me about six weeks before I could walk in any reasonable way and it took three to four months for me to get my voice back. The speech therapist used to come and see me once or twice a week and make me say, 'Threeee Bags . . . Bags . . . Bags . . . Of . . . Coal.' If you got it right she would say in her patronizing voice, 'Very good, James, well done.'

When I think back to that time a shiver goes down my spine. I think of what might have happened to me. Some of the other patients were given increased doses of Sulphonal. They turned into virtual zombies, drooling at the mouth and, like me, unable to walk; men, whom I'd seen in the past out playing football and being full of life, now shadows of their former selves. And to think that they, too, had their brains functioning and couldn't do anything about it.

After recovering from the Sulphonal treatment I progressed to being a patient orderly which I enjoyed. As at Murthly, I got great satisfaction from looking after my fellow patients, trying to improve the quality of their lives. During this time I did abscond a couple of times but only for the day to Glasgow and while this was frowned upon I didn't lose my privileges. The next time I absconded I went as far as London. I hitch-hiked my way from Glasgow to London and ended up at Victoria. There I found out about a place that looks after those down on their luck. It's run by Catholic Sisters and it's still there to this day. Anybody

74

can go in and have a wash and a meal and if their feet are bad there's a chiropodist to do their feet for them. They were so kind to everyone. 'Do you feel you want a bath?' they'd ask. 'Do you want a couple of aspirins?' 'Do you want us to wash your clothes while you're having a bath?' They allowed you to sleep in easy chairs during the day if you wanted to but the place closed at ten at night and wasn't open again until about five in the morning. At night I would go to Victoria station. No-one bothered you there. There were always lots of people milling around. Anyway I had been fed well, bathed and had my feet done so I felt all right. I did think about trying to get a job but with no change of clothes and the fact that you usually have to pay two or three weeks' rent in advance in London I didn't think I stood much of a chance of succeeding. To get a job, apart from having presentable clothes, in those days you were expected to give an address to prove that you weren't a fly-by-night person.

Eventually I was so damn tired not having slept for three nights that I walked into the local police station and asked them for a bed for the night. 'What's your game, where are you from?' was the first reaction. I wasn't quick enough to tell them some cock-and-bull story so I just blurted out my own name and that I had absconded from Gartloch. Actually they were very good to me and gave me something to eat and some tea while they phoned Glasgow and arranged for two nurses to come down to collect me. The next morning Joe and Donald came to pick me up and take me back by train. On the journey Donald asked if it would be all right for us to eat in the dining carriage. Joe said it would be OK as long as Donald got a receipt. We had lunch and high tea and the service was exceptional. I thought that the waiter would get a good tip from Donald at the end but when Donald asked for a receipt he handed him a shilling. 'Oh no, I couldn't, sir,' said the waiter, who was fuming. 'All right,' said Donald and put the shilling back in his pocket.

When we returned to Gartloch I was put back into the admission ward. They were angry at me and told me that they were going to put me on a new treatment again to 'help' me. That treatment was to be ECT – electroconvulsive therapy. At Gartloch they were very stupid and uncaring about the way they gave you the electro treatment. Those who were ready to receive it were taken to a small ante-room outside the main operating theatre. You put on gowns which tied down the back and you were made to wait. There were four of us waiting just outside the swing doors of the theatre when I heard this blood-curdling scream. I didn't know what to think. It scared the living daylights out of me. I leapt up and ran along the corridor as fast as I could and out of the first door that I could with all the nurses chasing after me. Eventually they caught me on the football pitch and took me back. I was screaming when they brought me back. I was in terror. I don't think I have ever been so afraid in my life. They put me on a trolley and covered me with a sheet which they rolled together at the sides with the one underneath. I learned later the reason for their leaving the top sheet loose. In those days there was no pre-med given before electro treatment. While today it's not used so much the patients are given a pre-med. What happens is that your head is dampened and two pieces of metal, called headphones, are attached to the side of your head at the temples. If you have false teeth they take them out; I had all my own teeth. Then you are given a rubber stick to bite on. So you are lying there not knowing what's going to happen next. After a couple of sessions I knew what would happen which made it even worse. In the corner of the room sat one of the doctors with what for all the world looked like a wireless set with dials on it. This was for varying the charge. When the doctor nodded the nurse took the two wires with their bare ends and placed them on the metal discs attached to your head. Then there is one almighty flash. You never forget it. I have not forgotten it to this day. The next thing you remember after the blinding flash is waking up in bed back in the ward. Each time I was given the treatment I would plead with them not to give it to me. 'I *will* be good, I promise I won't run away again,' I would scream, but to no avail.

In all I had twelve sessions of electro treatment in courses of three. After each course you have a 'resting' period, which only prolongs the agony. They used to bring certain patients from all the wards and at the end of the day the staff would be saying, 'That was a good day today.' One day before the treatment I mentioned the screaming to Captain Gordon with the result that I was left to the last and kept in the ward. I don't know what was worse: hearing the screams or waiting for them to come and get you.

Just before the third treatment I grabbed hold of Captain Gordon and pleaded with him to make them stop it. I gave him all the promises. I do believe he was sincere but he told me it was for my own good. While the flash horrified me, the fact that I knew when it was going to come, by the doctor's nodding, was petrifying. It was a barbaric treatment. What kind of fiendish mind invented something like that? And the reason for the sheets being left loose? This was because the body would rise up three, sometimes four, feet in the air when the shock was administered. In the old days the patients were strapped in tight and apparently some ended up breaking their back or their neck when the body reacted to the shock and had no room to move.

I found out later that the way the nursing staff gauged whether or not the blast had penetrated was by one watching your feet during the blast. If your toes turned in they would say, 'That was a good one, that was a beauty.'

A few weeks after the last session I ran away again. I thought I had to get out of that place but with no money where could I go? What could I do? So I returned to the hospital. I was then called into the Medical Superintendent's office. He picked up a letter from his desk and said that it had come from the Procurator-Fiscal in Glasgow, who expressed concern that I had been in a position to escape from the hospital six or seven times and stated that if it happened again I would be taken back to court. 'It's up to you now, Jimmy,' said the Superintendent. 'One more mistake and you're in real trouble.'

For a while things went well. I was working away in the old people's ward looking after them. One day I began to realize, again, that here I was doing the same job as a nurse. If I'm fit to do this then I can't be stupid. At that time I was doing exactly the same tasks as a nurse: making beds, changing the old men, feeding those who couldn't feed themselves. In return for all this I was given twenty cigarettes by the charge nurse. In fact, this charge nurse regularly wanted away at five o'clock to play bowls, instead of staying on until eight-thirty. On his bowling night he would come to me and ask me to cover for him while he went bowling. A charge nurse saying to me, a patient, could I stay on!

But psychiatrists don't want to know how well you're doing. They have a different perception of the whole thing. If I had mentioned the nursing incident to one of them he would say that just showed how much the charge nurse trusted me, or how capable I was. Indeed, I should have been *grateful* to work those hours on behalf of the charge nurse.

While Gartloch was an improvement on places like Murthly the barbaric form of treatment was unforgivable. As drugs were being tried out, so

I believe, we were being treated as guinea-pigs. No doubt it would be claimed that it would be not only for our benefit but for future generations of patients. Psychiatric medicine was still in the dark ages in those days and I was unfortunate to be among the patients at that time. To judge by the types of questions you were asked at a psychoanalysing session, they had been decided, no doubt, by some eminent professor who probably had never sat down and talked to a mentally ill patient, man to man, to try and find out, simply by talking, what was in his mind. Mental patients were regarded as subnormal no matter what degree of mental illness the patient had. Having spent, by this time, over sixteen years in mental institutions I discovered that the system hadn't changed and would not change until mental patients were seen as individuals and not as a collective group to be the subject of experiments.

6

From Patient to Inmate

When I was sent from Barlinnie Prison to Gartloch Hospital I was under Section 23:2(b), which meant that I could be recalled to court if I committed an offence or if my conduct was not up to standard in any way. I had been told by the Medical Superintendent that I was on my last warning and that should I abscond again I'd be in real trouble. Although I realized that running away would return me to court I still had to go. I wasn't really getting anywhere at Gartloch. I was in a trusted position as a patient nurse but that wasn't good enough for me. I wanted out. But there was no way in the system which existed at that time. It wasn't as if they told you that you were progressing and if you continued then you would be getting out, or even considered for release after a certain amount of time. I know that, unlike a broken leg which doctors can predict the length of time it will take to heal, there is no way that a doctor can predict how long it will take to cure someone who is mentally ill, but they could try to give you some hope.

I don't know whether or not I wanted to prove to them that their threat of 'real trouble' didn't mean anything to me but one day not long after the Superintendent's warning I went off again. It really was futile. I almost knew that all I would do was get to Glasgow, wander around and then come back again. Maybe if I had been able to go out on a trust basis to Glasgow then I wouldn't have kept absconding. Who knows? When I returned I found it strange that the Superintendent didn't ask to see me. I became suspicious that something was wrong. My suspicions were proved right. The next day, Saturday, I was taken up before a Sheriff and the Procurator-Fiscal. Once again I had a 'poor man's lawyer', a different one this time. He didn't say a thing. The Procurator-Fiscal went on about my running away and that as I was under Section 23:2(b), 'It has been decided to send you to Perth where you can get treatment to make you better.' My appearance was brief. In all it took about five minutes. The Sheriff asked if I, the patient, would be going away for a short time. 'Oh yes, My Lord,' said the Procurator-Fiscal, 'he's only going to be there until he's better.' Better — that was the laughable side of it.

That was it. I was taken downstairs by two plain-clothes policemen who took me from there to the Criminal Lunatic Department (CLD) at Perth. I wasn't even given a chance to say anything at the appearance. I was supposedly unfit to plead.

And it wasn't just my case. There are times when people could plead and they are told not to say anything. 'We'll do all the talking for you. Don't you say anything,' they would order. This is where a lot goes unsaid in court when it should be brought out in the open and the 'patient' given a chance to put his case. But it's a case of 'Let's get it all over and done with quickly.' Almost like a backdoor method of justice. It's an old, old story. 'He's not well enough and anyway I don't think he'll cause us any trouble. He's no threat to our practising "justice". He's only a blot on the landscape.' That's certainly the way I, and many others, feel about it. I am sure that I could have given a good account of myself if I had been allowed to speak but I am equally sure that it had all been decided beforehand.

As I was being taken to Perth I thought, 'This is the end for me.' The very address: Criminal Lunatic Department, Perth. What can I say? I was very frightened. And all this had come about following one outburst after a traumatic two days in Glasgow. How I regretted that outburst.

When we arrived I was handed over at the gate. What a forbidding place it looked. I remembered that I had passed the place on one of my trips out of Murthly and it looked a hellish place from the outside. Now I was about to find out what it was like on the inside. I was received at the desk by the chief officer of the CLD, taken away, stripped, bathed and put into Room 3. They never called them cells but they were. There was a mattress on the floor, sheets and blankets. You lay there for three days until they got to know you. The next day a doctor came in. All he said was, 'Oh yes.' That was all, just 'Oh yes.' No question of asking why I was there or anything like that.

It was a cold impersonal place. When I compared the admission routine to that of Gartloch it was like chalk and cheese. The warders, as everyone called them – there were no nurses – were mostly rejects from the normal prison system. If any of them had fouled up, as regards behaviour, at another prison they were sent to the CLD. Shoved out of the way. The daily routine was very similar to that operated in mental institutions. You got up at six-thirty, washed and had breakfast which was always porridge, bread and a cup of tea. There was an exercise yard which was open all day and you could go out there when you wanted. There was therapy of sorts, but the main therapy was working in the garden. I scrubbed floors. That was the first job for new patients. While it was boring and repetitive you managed to get through each day. There was the odd bit of friendly banter with the warders, then there was the other type, very much the prison officer. Not for him the use of the Christian name. 'I am Mr so and so,' he would say. So you learned which ones to call Mister and the ones you could call by their first name.

The other inmates were a mixed bag. There were murderers, rapists, child molesters and some who had been in there for a very long time. There was one who had been in since the Thirties. He was quite an old man. Even though they said that he could leave he had refused. He was living in cloud-cuckoo-land and had made himself a king. He was a GPI, that is, he suffered from general paralysis of the insane. It comes from being in contact with someone who has syphilis. People like him usually end up thinking themselves to be a king or a queen. They are quite convinced and they are set in their ways. He was quite a character. He was even allowed to wear a soft hat of his own. In the CLD that is quite a privilege. He was also allowed to wear his own clothes whereas the rest of us had to wear prison clothing. As far as the child molesters were concerned, they quickly cut out a niche for themselves. They knew that they were going to be inside for a long time. Unlike the normal prison system, they were not harassed or beaten up by other inmates. Nobody ever commented on or spoke about anyone else's crime. That was the unwritten law in the CLD. Even if you lost your temper at someone and started castigating someone about their crime you would be shouted down by the other inmates.

It was at the CLD that I learned about self-preservation. The first rule is don't fall foul of the staff. They won't bother you if you don't bother them. As long as you are there at the count then you're all right. There were three counts a day. Everyone stood still and in each area the head man would go round and count the inmates. Once everyone had checked with their individual totals the chief officer would shout, 'Let them go', and we'd start wandering around again. I only once fell foul of the staff when I refused to pull the plough.

They used to harness six patients on to a plough to plough the fields at the CLD. I found this abhorrent and reminiscent of slavery. I refused to do it and was locked up for three days and given large doses of castor oil. Times reminiscent of the Crutin Oil they gave us at Baldovan. It was their answer to obstinacy. When you were locked up you were put in a cell within a cell. It was called the 'back end'. You were completely out of contact with the rest of the inmates. You just lay there for three days. There was the odd warder who would slip you a cigarette. I dare say that they liked to get through the day as smoothly as possible. These were the humane ones. I have always been convinced, during my time in mental institutions, that the chief warder would put some good warders in along with the bad ones. I would look down the roster of warders at the CLD and I would see the good and bad split up. That made life a little more tolerable. You knew that if certain ones were on you would get another cigarette or an extra slice of bread at teatime.

The layout of the CLD was that of a prison hall. There were about a hundred inmates there. The ground floor was divided into four sections. There was a TV room, a dining room, a kitchen area and a wireless room. The smoking room was the biggest area, stone pillars and the like. Everyone walked up and down there. There were no chairs. The cells were all upstairs. They didn't have prison doors as such but they were secure. The cells had large windows – unlike prison cells – but with bars.

The routine was very strict. You had to make

a request to see the doctor even though he came through the hall every day. You were not allowed to stop him on his way past. Once you went inside his office you saluted him and then told him what was wrong with you. Obviously in an institution for the criminally insane there were problems. Almost every night you'd hear windows being smashed and the culprits being severely dealt with by the warders. There were regular fights but there were also 'mixers', or grasses. We had one particular person who would create trouble and then just as the trouble reached boiling point he tipped off the staff that something was going to happen. Just as it was about to blow he would be put in bed for, say, being insolent to the staff. There was also violence involving the staff. One of the assistant chief officers was particularly handy with his fists. One day we were sitting in the wireless room and he went over to one of the troublemakers and said, 'Come here, son, I want to ask you something.' As the inmate rose he gave him one on the chin – a real haymaker. The inmate was carted off to the 'back end' and we found out later that the beating continued.

These beatings weren't just out of malice, they were also used to keep the troublemakers and grasses cowed. And it worked. We had a black chap arrive at the CLD as an inmate. He was always talking about escaping. One summer's evening the mist came down over the exercise yard and the warders hadn't noticed it coming. In the ensuing panic to get the inmates inside the black chap slipped away. Following the head-count the sirens and escape bells went off. They found him in a hen-run near the wall. The person who grassed on him was the one who had collected a haymaker on the chin a few days earlier. Yet it didn't do him any good. He regularly got thumped about by the warders. I think that while he was useful to them, they actually despised him.

Of the hundred or so inmates in the CLD almost half of them shouldn't have been there at all. It was the case then, and still is today, that pleading insanity or diminished responsibility will get you a term in a mental institution rather than in prison. I am convinced that those who committed very serious crimes such as child molesting and child murders were advised to plead insanity and then they did a term at the CLD. While there were inmates who had been there for a very long time, it wasn't the case that no-one ever got out. There were one or two releases every year and when that time came along it was the event of the year. They were invariably released to a centre in Dundee whether or not the inmate came from Dundee. First, the inmate worked in a Salvation Army hostel in Dundee then he would be allowed out on probation under a probation officer from Edinburgh. There was no psychiatric treatment at the CLD. It was the days of castor oil, bromide and paraldehyde. There was no question of their trying to cure you. Their way of making you 'better' was to break you or to numb your mind into submission. If an inmate came in as a violent case the authorities' answer was to fill him full of drugs, beat the violence out of him or put him on a course of excessive purgatives. It amused me to think that the authorities believed that they could remove the 'badness' from an inmate by making him sit on a toilet pan for hours on end. That was the level of mental health care in the CLD.

As at Baldovan and Murthly and even at Gartloch, there was no redress for inmates. At the CLD we were allowed to petition the Secretary of State for Scotland for a review of our case. First, you asked for permission to see the doctor and then asked him for permission to have a petition. 'Yes, certainly,' he would reply. You wrote your petition on an official blue sheet of paper complete with instructions on it. 'The inmate will not write below this line and the inmate will use only one side of the paper. If two sheets are required then the inmate will request to be permitted to use two sheets of paper.' In my petition I would write that I felt that my stay was unnecessary and that it was not helpful to me whatsoever. The petition would be addressed to the Secretary of State at St Andrew's House but you always had your answer within twenty-four hours. It really was one big con. The day after you had handed in your petition for posting you would be summoned to the doctor's office and he would seem to have an official letter in front of him which he kept folded towards him in case you saw it, and he would tell you that your petition had been refused. No reason given at all. I don't believe that our petitions ever left the CLD. How on earth they thought that we would believe that a letter posted in Perth one day could be replied to by the next, I don't know. Even if it had been posted it would hardly have arrived in Edinburgh by the next day. It was all part of the game which we, of course, played along with even though we knew it wouldn't get us anywhere. As they say, we may be daft but we're not stupid!

Although the CLD was part of Perth Prison and we had warders instead of nurses the doctor was the figurehead. From a medical point of view he was a loathsome man. He showed loathing towards almost everyone but in particular to the child molesters. He prescribed a particular type of tablet for them that was to remove their sexual urges and he took great delight in bringing the molesters into his surgery and putting them through a degrading process. They would be made to drop their trousers and then he would play with their genitals to see if they could get an erection. They couldn't, of course, after taking the tablets.

As the years went on at the CLD my own life improved a little. We were encouraged in the wintertime to put on plays with the help of the Perth Theatre. We were also allowed to take the plays out to other mental hospitals. The winter went very quickly. The summer seemed to drag. I read a lot of books, particularly A. J. Cronin. A warder had given me one of them one day and then continued to supply me with others. You also made your own entertainment, but the main thing was to keep out of trouble. Don't get involved. Unlike my time in Baldovan, Murthly and Gartloch, you daren't interfere or dream of saying, 'Oh, that's wrong', or 'You shouldn't do that'. No, you kept your eyes open and your mouth shut. The warders at the CLD were a law unto themselves. The Prison Governor came through each day and we all had to salute him. No inmate in the CLD was allowed to approach him. We were outwith his area. One poor soul did decide to complain to the Governor one morning saying that the warders were treating him badly and that he shouldn't be in the CLD. The Governor just stared at him. I cringed when I heard him complain, I knew what would happen next. He was taken in to the 'back end' and came out well bruised. He had obviously fallen and hurt himself while in the 'back end'. It's quite extraordinary how often the mental patient hurts himself, in the oddest places too!

I found the years I spent at the CLD a great strain mentally. While I'm not saying that I reckoned myself any better than the other inmates, when I consider the heinous crimes which they had committed and my only 'crime' had originally been a breach of the peace and then the absconding, I knew I shouldn't be there. A ray of hope came into my life for a short period when the psychiatrist in charge of the mental defectives at Carstairs came up to see the inmates who were soon to be transferred to the newly designated State Hospital. Doctor Bruce was his name. He was the one whose son was badly beaten and stuffed in a foxhole by one of the mental defectives at Carstairs. After interviewing me, he said, 'Why is this man in here? We'll have to get him out of here.' I was elated. At long last someone understood me. Time went on and I heard nothing. I found out later that he had died not long after seeing me.

I suppose what kept me going, as it has always done, was the knowledge that I was not criminally insane and that sometime I would be back in the outside world again. I learned to tread warily, be prepared for the unexpected and when the unexpected arrived be ready with my answer. As an example, we would be sitting in the wireless room, some playing chess, some sleeping and some just listening to the wireless. Suddenly six or seven warders would come rushing in. They would be looking for something or someone who had committed a misdemeanour and anyone else involved in it. They'd put us up against the wall and say, 'Right you, what do you know about so and so?' If you didn't have the right answer you were automatically considered guilty. But if you could look them in the face, not in an insubordinate way, of course, and say that you knew nothing about the incident then you were let away. There were various things they were looking for: details of planned escapes, thefts and instances of arson. Arson was quite a problem at the CLD. Usually it was just malicious like setting fire to rubbish bins but on one occasion the whole place almost burned down. One of the inmates gave one of the easily led inmates a rag soaked in 3 in 1 oil and some matches and told him to put the rag into a hole in the wall in his cell. He told him that if his cell was damaged they'd give him a better cell. The walls of the cell were not concrete, like prison, but made with an asbestos-type material about three inches thick. The lad did so at night and the resultant fire almost burned the whole place down. Fortunately there were no lives lost. When the blaze started the warders were in such a panic. Not only didn't they know how to treat mental illness they didn't seem to know how to extinguish a fire!

I have said that you kept your mouth shut at the CLD and didn't interfere when something wrong was going on. It wasn't only beatings I have in mind. It was the little, simple things, hardly worth bothering about, that affected me as well. A cigarette is money both in prison and at places like the CLD. All our cigarettes came in large trunks from the Customs. They were invariably American cigarettes like Camel and Pall Mall. They came in their thousands supposedly for everyone. But you still had to go up to a warder and ask for permission to get a cigarette. Why didn't they just hand them out? Some, of course, managed to get more than their share.

Another bad thing was the way that the doctor had his favourites. I didn't dislike the inmates who were his favourites but I hated the fact that there were any at all. He'd have a list of people whom he'd take out for runs in his car but sometimes he'd turn them down at the last minute just to prove that he was in charge of their lives. He got his just desserts, though. He went insane himself and ended up in Murray Royal Hospital, ironically being nursed by mental patients. His attitude fitted in with the warders' way, of course. Anything that happened, happened behind closed doors. While a report, called a 'harsh sheet', would be made out following an incident it usually took the form of 'As I approached inmate Jones he put his hand up as if to strike me. In an attempt to restrain him the inmate sustained a black eye', or 'While trying to restrain the inmate he fell and hit his head on the door handle.'

I say, again, there was brutality and too much of it; particularly in the 'back end', the silent area. Cut off from the rest of the CLD where no-one could hear your screams. But everyone knew. And the strange thing was that when you were let out of the 'back end' after a beating you were given twenty cigarettes. This wasn't to keep your mouth shut. It was already shut. It was as if they were saying, 'We're sorry but it was necessary.'

Surprisingly, and thank God for it, there was no evidence of homosexuality in our section of the CLD. I was glad of that. I did fear at one time that with everyone cooped up there it would be rampant. But there was a ring of homosexuality in the 'new' division where we weren't allowed. This is where they kept the 'key' patients, 'trusted' patients. A lot of it went on there until there was a big bust-up and one chap tried to commit suicide. It was all covered up, of course.

While I was there I was the only one without crimes hanging over my head. That was until we were about to be transferred to Carstairs, then they began flowing in from all over the country. People being put out of the way. The place became a dumping ground for the people whom the other hospitals couldn't cope with or weren't interested in. As I have said there was no redress in those days; no-one to speak up for you – unlike today, when MPs and others will demand investigations into the problems at mental institutions. All you had to rely on – and I smile when I say rely on – was the powers that be. They may sympathize with you, laugh with you and sometimes weep with you but that was all. You were just a number. In my case 56. Everything connected with me was 56. At times I was happy, at times depressed. But you had to have strength and intelligence. These were the qualities which saw you through. You carried on as far as you were allowed. You never crossed the line that was your boundary.

7

Another New Start

About two years before we were transferred to the
State Hospital at Carstairs nurses from all over
the country began arriving at the CLD. They were
there to get to know us before we went to Carstairs. There was one particular chap from Cornhill
Hospital in Aberdeen who was very concerned that
there were no daily reports or messages left when
staff changed over shifts. At Cornhill they had a
system operating whereby each staff change-over
would report the goings on to the staff taking over.
So he went to the chief warder and asked to start
a daily report on each inmate. The chief warder
replied, in front of all of us, 'There's never anything
like that bloody well here. Don't start your fucking
nonsense in here. Just you stand there and make sure
no one escapes! They get fed, they wander about
and then they go to their beds. That's the kind of
nursing you'll do while you're here.'

Slowly the old warders were scattered away to
the prison system and we were left with male nurses.

Until they were in the majority they were powerless to do any kind of nursing. The hatred of them by the warders was very obvious.

There was a great deal of anticipation in the air as the time drew close for our transfer to Carstairs. We were going to a 'real' hospital. How we were fooled! We were to find out that conditions in Carstairs at that time were just as bad as the CLD, as regards treatment. We were taken to Carstairs from Perth in a fleet of blue buses. We had a police escort who handed us over at each county to the next escort group. Eventually we arrived at Carstairs. There was a 'niceness' about it to begin with but that soon changed after we had been there for a few days. There were no charge nurses with any experience in the job. All those who had been at CLD were very young and while they had got to know us over the past two years they were suddenly put under charge nurses from the mental deficiency wing at Carstairs, the East Wing. These people knew nothing about us, but even so, they had obviously made up their minds on how they were going to deal with us.

Each Thursday night the charge nurse stood at the foot of the stairs with a large enamel pail of liquorice which was used as a purgative for bowel movement. Nobody had heard of it before and each person was given his dosage as he went up to bed. You see they still had this belief, as it is today, this *obsession* with bowel movements. They had to clean out the wickedness from you. This went on for about five weeks then people started refusing to take it and it was stopped. Well, at Carstairs you don't refuse to do anything. 'We're the ones in charge here,' the charge nurse would tell you, 'you're not at the CLD now.' But we had ways of getting back at them. The male nurses hated being called 'nurse'. I don't know why, they probably thought it was effeminate. So we always called them 'nurse'. When we were transferred from Perth the nurses had split us up into what they considered were the relative groups with regard to a patient's condition. The 'top' ward was H, L was a little lower and J and K were the lowest groups. Then there was Medwin ward which was for the very bad cases. When we left Perth there were three patients, I would say, who were candidates for Medwin. Within weeks Medwin was full. These patients just couldn't take the changes. They realized that their 'easy' life-style at the CLD, where we just all wandered around together, was changing. They had been separated from people they had been with, in some cases, for years. At Carstairs you were all in different blocks. You even exercised as a ward. There was no contact with other patients in other wards unless you were on the garden detail or in the laundry. So it was a big emotional upheaval, more so for the long-term men who had been in the CLD. It was mostly they who fell by the wayside. They seemed to lose their reason for going on, although it wasn't surprising. While the CLD was no paradise we were now being treated like dafties. Up in the morning, sweep out your room, don't go downstairs unless you're told, wash and then breakfast. All to the accompaniment of a nurse talking to you as if you were a child. 'Come on now, boys. Good boys. Oh, how smart we look today.' It was in the washroom that things sometimes boiled over. Those who wanted away from the regime and to be on their own in Medwin would suddenly turn on someone and say, 'Who the hell are you looking at?' A fight would start and they would get their wish . . . off to Medwin for a few days.

Very soon after we arrived a new doctor joined us: Dr Ross. He'd be in his early thirties. He was very progressive and had lots of good ideas. For example, he wanted to convert the small units near the bowling green for patients who were getting out to train them for freedom but the Board of Control said no. He also wanted us to have civilian clothes, again the Board wouldn't hear of it. Eventually he left.

The idea of civilian clothes would have been a good one as it would have made us look a little more 'normal'. We were still wearing the parish tweeds – grey tweed and blue tweed – at least they weren't all grey as worn at the CLD – and we wore a green and white striped shirt. You got as near a fit as possible. There was no question of measuring your chest or your waist. If you were lucky enough and were first in the queue you got the pick of the bunch. There were some odd-looking sights who ended up at the back of the queue and got what was left.

At that period the sanction which was put on you if you stepped out of line was to remove a privilege which they had given you. At the CLD they didn't allow inmates to have their own radios.

At Carstairs you could have one bought for you by your family or if you had the money the authorities would buy it for you. However, the radio was the first thing to go if you misbehaved. They used it as a polite form of blackmail. 'Now you realize you're only getting this if you behave yourself,' the nurses would say. 'Don't forget we can take it away anytime we want to.' That was the degrading part and the reason I never bothered with a radio for years. I wouldn't give them the satisfaction of blackmailing me with it. What angered me then was that often I just wanted to sit down and have an intelligent conversation with someone: not about the hospital but about something topical which had, say, been in the papers. That was frowned upon. You weren't allowed to be intelligent. If you did start a conversation with one of the nurses within minutes it would turn to, 'Oh, I see what's his name got locked up today.' I hated that. I'll be honest though, I don't think many of them could have had an intelligent conversation.

In the first few years there was no improvement in the therapeutic treatment. There were new drugs though, which no doubt the system considered to be an improvement on the previous ones. Once again it was trial and error. The great new 'cure-all' was the tranquillizing drug Largactil. That kept them down! It also gave you what we called the Largactil kick. You would see a group of men sitting in a room and all of them would be kicking their feet up involuntarily. Another was Fentazin, which made you walk round all day with your head to the side. 'Don't worry, it'll wear off,' they would say. It didn't. The next thing that happened was when the authorities in their wisdom decided to employ auxiliaries. I remember the advert in the *Scotsman* for nursing staff for a progressive hospital: 'Only those of the highest calibre need apply.' We were lucky when we got one out of the new intake. There was a chap came from England, Alan Cheatham was his name, and he brought up his wife and family to Carstairs. He thought he was coming to a progressive hospital, after all that's what the advert had said. One day he went up to the charge nurse after the garden party had left, and a group of five and I were cleaning the ward. 'Once they've finished in here will they be starting the group therapy?' he asked. 'The only group therapy you'll have is to stand at your station and see that nobody gets out.' Shades of the CLD. You see the problem was that those who had been at the CLD had been indoctrinated into the prison mentality, 'confine and contain', and they then continued this at Carstairs. All their original ideas that they may have had had been knocked out of them by the system. Brutality was also in evidence from very early on; back to the old-fashioned idea that they could *beat* the wickedness out of you.

When the ordinary mental hospitals began to use Carstairs as a dumping ground the situation worsened. These hospitals were becoming more progressive in their methods and didn't want the old lags around so they sent them to us. Among those to arrive was a chap from Edinburgh, big

Jimmie. He was an impulsive character. He got beaten up so many times he was always on the defensive. On one occasion three nurses were standing talking when Jimmie went by and one of them made some nasty remark to him. He went to take a swing at them. One nurse saw it coming and ducked and the others grabbed hold of Jimmie and gave him the kicking of his life. They eventually cowed him into submission but not before a particular nurse had given him a few more goings over. Not by himself, you understand, always with three or four others. That particular nurse has now retired – a good thing for Carstairs. He was not even liked by his fellow nurses but they could do nothing about him. I came across him once when I had asked to go to Medwin ward. It seems strange to ask to go into what was classed as the lowest-level ward but there you were on your own and I found it good to get away from everyone for a few days.

I had fallen and hurt my hip while in Medwin – my own fault, I can assure you! When breakfast was brought round I was unable to get out of bed.

'Right,' says this nurse. 'Refusing breakfast.'

I said, 'Hang on a minute, I can't move, I've hurt my hip.'

He slammed the door shut. Later, when I did manage to move, I rang the bell in the room and the heavy-handed nurse arrived. 'What the hell do you want now?' he asked.

'Can I have my breakfast now, please?'

'You refused it before, you're now on report.' That's the way they treated you.

The next day being Friday was room-cleaning and inspection day. Again I was accused of refusing breakfast and when they came round to check my room I was still in bed. I said that I couldn't move. 'Right, we'll sort this out,' says the nurse. 'Put him in the padded cell and get someone else to clean his room.' I should have been in the padded cell for only a few minutes but they let me lie there for three hours. I decided that I wasn't going to let them get away with that and I asked the charge nurse for a piece of paper and an envelope to write and complain to the doctor. My letter caused a bit of a stink. Seemingly the charge nurse was unaware of what had happened. Dr Neville came to me and said — as have other doctors over the years — 'I know, but they'll deny it.' In those days other patients wouldn't act as a witness for a patient. They valued their hide too much. In truth that wasn't the only reason. Life would be made very tough for them if they acted as witness against a nurse and they would be subjected to mental cruelty. For example, they might ask for a packet of cigarettes from their property and the nurse would tell them that they would give it to him when they wanted to. Then they would have to wait for two or three days. But while Dr Neville was unable to do anything about that case he did have me taken back to my own ward away from that particularly brutal nurse.

At that time, the staff ran the show, not the doctors. In many ways it's still the case now as the doctors have to rely on the staff but they have more influence over the nurses today. The doctors were there as figureheads. They would come in and ask, 'How's Jimmy Laing today?' 'Oh, I think he needs some more Largactil, doctor,' the nurse would say. 'It's been a great help to him.' What they meant was that it had given them an easy life with us sitting around in a docile way. The doctor would agree to an increase in the dosage without even checking the patient. Dr Neville did try eventually to get group meetings going in the top wards to discuss, with the patients, benefits which we should have and the treatment we were getting, but all this was very superficial. He never got down to the real problem.

There had been a fracas in Pentland ward in the East Wing when three mental defectives had attacked a charge nurse at his desk. The alarms went off and they were put upstairs and locked in. Now the routine if a patient like this was locked up was that he didn't get his fried breakfast. He got porridge, a little milk and watery tea. They scrubbed floors all day, back and forwards, over and over again. They were then put on tablets to calm them down. At lunchtime they were again locked up and given soup and bread. What was happening though was that one of the nurses was taking their evening meal up to them and shouting at them, 'Look what you could be having if you behaved yourselves.' Then he would take it away. This went on time after time. Even though they were getting tablets this was driving them to distraction. Dr Neville heard about this and wanted to charge the nurse with mental cruelty but no-one would back him up. He even wanted to reprimand the nurse but the Scottish Prison Officers Association (SPOA), the union the nurses belonged to, wouldn't allow it. It showed how powerful the union was. I always thought it was a contradiction in terms that we were in a hospital being looked after by 'nurses' and yet they were members of the Scottish Prison Officers Association.

Dr Neville did try to help me though. He told me, 'You know, someone made a hell of a mistake over you.' It was good to hear but nothing came of it. He wasn't there long enough to be able to do anything about my case. It must be understood that things move very slowly at places like Carstairs. It's not a case that one doctor thinks you shouldn't be there and then you get out.

I did repay his concern for me. I did it because, as I have said, I have principles tucked away in my back pocket. You always have them although you can't always use them. This time I was able to. There was a patient in Carstairs from Dumfries. He was in for rape. He always pled his innocence and Dr Neville was coming round to thinking that it was true. I was working in the kitchen of our ward one day when I overheard him and another patient discussing the next visit of his wife. They were planning that after the visit his wife would go and see Dr Neville who, as usual, would be on his own, and that after she was in his office for a few minutes she would start screaming and tearing her dress to make it look as if Dr Neville had attacked her. This, they felt, would be covered up and the Dumfries man would be released.

I informed the charge nurse and he told Dr Neville. On the day before the visit Dr Neville came to our ward and asked to see me and the chap from Dumfries. I was asked to repeat the story. It was fairly nerve-racking but the charge nurse told me that the Dumfries man would be transferred that day. I repeated my story in front of both the patient and Dr Neville. 'Well, what do you have to say to all that?' Neville asked the patient. 'Oh, it wasn't my idea, it was the other chap's idea.' 'Do you know,' said Neville, 'I was quite convinced of your innocence? You have now given me great cause to think otherwise.'

On the Saturday there were three charge nurses in Dr Neville's office when the wife came in so the plan failed. Since then that patient has been released but later he was murdered. Dr Neville came to me later and thanked me personally. Yet, he never inquired as to why I had done it. It probably never occurred to him that I had principles, he no doubt thought that I was currying favour with him or the charge nurse.

At Carstairs there was a minority of bad staff, but they were a very strong minority; to such an extent that even the majority who were either good or harmless were under their control and sometimes fell in with their ways. When you have a group of people who are confined and have no real power of redress it is very easy for such staff to get their own way with the patients. In other words they can do or say what they want to you. For some time I, like the rest of the patients, had been suffering the mental cruelty which was practised by the staff. Egging us on, geeing us up, as they called it. In my particular case, I was walking past two of them one day, they were standing just outside the office, and just as I passed them one would say to the other, 'Look at that bastard. You're right, you know, he is a right bastard.' Then there would be little innuendoes.

I thought, 'That's it. I'm going to do something about this.' I went to the charge nurse on duty and told him that I was fed up with all the egging on. I told him what had happened over the previous months. 'Right, Jimmy,' he said, 'it's about time a stop was put to this. I've heard all this before. The Assistant Chief will be in soon and we'll talk to him.' Fergus Findlay, the Assistant Chief, was a very fair man, one of the few. He said that he would talk to them individually. First he brought the staff nurse involved into the office. I tried to listen but couldn't hear. Later I was told he admitted it. Then he brought in the enrolled nurse who had also been involved. He totally denied the incident but when he was told that his staff nurse had admitted to it he confessed. This really was a feather in my cap that they had admitted going over the score. Had they both denied it I would probably have been 'sorted out'. The staff nurse was given a dressing down as was the enrolled nurse and they were split up.

One might think that this would have made me a target for further treatment. The reverse was the case. They realized that I was no mug and I was treated with a bit more 'care'. While that was an example of some form of redress and my 'standing' had gone up, if you wanted to survive in Carstairs you had to be a good cheat, a thief and a liar. Carstairs was really like a prison and, like a prison, they supposedly prepared you for outside life, showing you how to behave in an upstanding way. But that was miles away from the truth of Carstairs. Through the Fifties and Sixties you had to learn to survive by whatever means. Later, things improved but at that time there was no accent on the therapeutic side of mental health. After all, considering the types of patient who were there, they were damned from the minute they entered. Yet if they had tried to understand us they would have got on better. But that was not to be, not for a few years.

After my complaint had been successfully upheld my life in Carstairs improved. I still had my follies but I got away with them. Perhaps my complaint also led to others being able to get away with the odd thing as well. It wasn't a comfortable position to be in. For a while after, the staff were almost wary of me. 'Oh Christ, if you do that to him we'll be in the bloody soup,' I once overheard.

The staff really were of such low calibre in those days that it was easy to get on their good side. I remember even writing for jobs for some of them. How they passed their nursing examinations mystifies me.

8

Carstairs: Ten Years On

In the mid-Sixties medicine was the answer to everything at Carstairs. Everybody was on one kind of a medicine or another. And the more you shouted, 'I shouldn't be on this,' the more they gave you. Fortunately I didn't go under as far as some did. I remember one nurse, an Irishman, who told me that I was getting enough to knock out a horse. I wasn't particularly trying to fight it, I just managed to get through it.

It was at that time that I fell and sustained a severe cut on my chin. They started to worry about me. One of the sweetest things that ever happened in my life, apart from eventually getting out, was the day Dr Neville said that he was concerned about me and that he was going to reduce my dosage of medicine. 'Oh no you're not,' was my reply. 'I either stay on the lot or come off it altogether.' I came off the lot. The withdrawal symptoms were horrendous. There were nights when I was falling off cliffs, drowning or walking through fire. I used to take three nightshirts – there were no pyjamas – to change overnight, owing to the sweating. During the day I was very snappy. The least little thing would set me off. But at the end of the day I conquered it. That showed me that I had the strength to overcome – inner strength. To be in that condition when I was on my own, locked up from seven at night until seven in the morning, with no-one to help me, I patted myself on the back at the end of it. No-one else did.

Around that time I had requested another transfer to Medwin ward, as I felt that I needed to get away from the daily routine after the traumas of the withdrawal from the drugs which I had been on. One morning I got up and was making my way to the washroom. On duty that morning was a charge nurse, two staff nurses and an enrolled nurse. As I approached Room 6 I heard a tremendous commotion. As I looked into Room 6 I saw the nurses were trying to restrain a patient. Restraining him? One of the staff nurses had a pillow over the patient's face and he was sitting on it. I said, 'For Christ's sake, you'll kill that guy!' The other staff nurse, who was the only good nurse on that day, shouted to his colleague, 'Come on, leave him, that's enough.' I then went onto the washroom and was mumbling away about that kind of particular treatment when the enrolled nurse came in and said, 'Right, Laing, shut up.' I said, 'No, I won't.' At that point, I still had my toothbrush in my hand. I hadn't even rinsed my mouth out. The nurse came towards me, rammed my arm up my back, and rushed me out of the washroom to my room. The pain was excruciating coupled with the fact that I was still holding my toothbrush which was digging into my back and pointing against the nurse. Suddenly it snapped and he screamed, 'Quick, he's trying to stab me!' Now, I ask you. How on earth could I stab him with one arm up behind my back with a broken toothbrush in my hand? When they threw me into the room I actually sat and wept. I hadn't done that for a long time but I felt so low. The charge nurse came in and offered me a cigarette. I said to him, 'Even you know that I'm not the kind of person who would stab someone. For Christ's sake, I had my arm up my back.'

'Och, don't worry about it, Jimmy,' he said. But I did. That was one thing I didn't want on my report card: James Laing has violent tendencies. There may have been many spots on my character but before then there was never any suggestion that I was violent. My concern was that if they considered me violent they would put me back on drugs supposedly in an attempt to calm me down. How I wished I had never seen the incident earlier on that morning.

About ten-thirty one of the doctors came round. He lay across the bottom of my bed and said, 'Why? Why, Jimmy?'

I said, 'There's obviously no use in talking to you about it because you're accepting the report.'

'I've seen the evidence, son,' he said, 'but you've not to worry, you didn't do anything. I'm sure the nurse won't hold it against you.' He pattered away and then we had a cigarette.

What should have happened was that he should have asked me, 'Did this happen or not?' When I said it didn't happen there should have been a full investigation. I was really perturbed about it. It would go down on my report as a violent outburst. Verbally I could always handle myself in a situation but once something was written down on your file there was no way of having it removed. Sure enough, when I got a chance to see my file about ten years later, I read it and it was there all right: Violent outburst, tried to stab a nurse. I was transferred out of Medwin ward twenty-four hours later – more proof that I didn't do anything. But it was on my file.

Around that time the black market at Carstairs began to operate. Everyone, including myself, smoked roll-ups, so tobacco was the hospital currency. If a member of the staff came into the store which I was in charge of to ask for, say, a pair of shoes, you would give him a pair without asking for anything. He would give you some tobacco 'for yourself'. Then it began to snowball. Each storeman in each ward had total charge of the patients' clothing requirements. The nursing staff did not interfere. You were left solely to your own devices. I always made sure that the patients came first and that they had the clothing they needed.

You received a 'floating' stock of shirts, shoes, underwear, pyjamas and the like. This was kept mainly for an emergency. If something was destroyed or went missing it was replaced from the floating stock and then a request would be made to the central stores for the further provision of the particular item. By manipulating the method of replacement I was able to build up the best stock of clothing in the hospital, to such an extent that sometimes the central stores would phone up and ask our charge nurse, 'Does Jimmy have any spare shirts?' Originally we had a weekly condemnation sheet when you would take any damaged or worn-out clothes down to the central stores. There were three storemen and if you were lucky enough to get the right one you just threw the bag of condemned clothes into the bin. The list of condemnations never tallied with what you had in the bag. You always put in for far more than you needed – just in case you had a 'customer' coming in. If you were unlucky enough to get one of the strict storemen, like Sid, who was very exact in his work, you would be made to check off everything you were claiming and if you were two pairs of shoes short you would say, 'Oh heck, I must have left them in the ward.' Of course, I had the two pairs back at the store but I was hoping to turn my stock into four pairs had he not noticed.

I felt that there must be a better system than risking being caught each time I wanted some extra supplies. I worked out that the best way would be to change the actual list of the condemnations. I filled out the particular form a couple of days before I was due to go to the central stores and then over the next days by touching an eraser to my tongue and then applying it to the list I would rub out the number of shirts and add in my own.

This never failed. If they had bothered to check the list carefully they would have been able to see the changes but fortunately they never did. If we had two shirts condemned one week I would rub out that number and make it three; never too many. There's no sense in trying to build up a large stock too quickly; easy does it.

The staff never checked the store, and the only time they would come in was to get something for themselves. One would come in needing a pair of flannels for his lad, 28-inch waist and 21-inch inside leg. The exchange rate for that would be two ounces of tobacco. One of the interesting things was that the staff rarely told one another that they were buying items, and I never told anyone, although they all knew that it was going on.

You would get one coming in and saying, 'I want a pair of flannels like the ones you gave Robbie.' I would reply, 'What on earth are you talking about?' There was one damn fool who came into my ward and asked the charge nurse if it was all right to ask me for a pair of shoes. 'I hear he's a good storeman,' he said. 'What are you on about?' the charge nurse replied. 'We don't do that sort of thing here – away you go.' Later the charge nurse came to me to tell me what had happened. 'You get some right fools in here among the staff,' he said. 'Very true,' I replied.

Eventually this particular nurse came back to the ward after the change of staff and asked for the pair of shoes. I told him that the deal was one ounce of tobacco and his old shoes back or two ounces without any shoes. He agreed but later he stupidly spoke to his father-in-law who was also a nurse and who said that the deal was a lot of nonsense and that he could get the shoes for nothing as I didn't pay for them. He came back to me and told me that this should be the case. I told him to get lost and that that was the deal. I knew that I could get the back-up of certain other nurses to help me, which I did. One of them told him that he would spoil it for everyone else if he didn't play the game. That was the kind of influence I had in Carstairs. I was ensnared in the system. They, themselves, in turn, had fallen into the ways of the system.

In the East Wing where the mental defectives were housed the set-up was different. As I have said before, mental defectives always want to be of good report and in the East Wing all the nurses had to do was to tell the storemen that they would get a good report and they could get the clothes they wanted. One might think that the nurses on our side could join in with that set-up but the mental defectives weren't so daft. One of our nurses tried it and the storeman let him away with it, or so he thought. After he had left the wing the patient went to the charge nurse and asked to see the report that this particular nurse had put in about him. 'What are you on about? You know that he doesn't work here,' said the charge nurse. 'Well,' said the patient, 'he told me that he was putting in a good report about me when I gave him the pair of shoes.'

All hell broke loose. I was asked by one of the nurses to supply a pair of shoes which went to replace the ones obtained in the East Wing and the nurse in question was made to pay up the two ounces of tobacco to me. He never tried to cheat the set-up again.

I instigated a grapevine system among the storemen. The nurse who had tried to tell me that he wasn't going to pay for the shoes was kept out of the set-up until he decided to come round and pay the rate required. He came back with the ounce of tobacco and his old shoes. He was let back into the set-up and I passed the word around. All you had to say was, 'Give so and so nothing.' That was it, you didn't have to expand on it. The other storemen knew.

The staff certainly knew how to take advantage of our set-up. One of the charge nurses was going on holiday and I rigged him out from head to toe. He told me when he returned that he had gone into the pub in Carnwath that evening and that another nurse had complimented him on his outfit. 'By God, you're looking suave tonight.' He had been wearing what I supplied. Beige trousers, checked jacket, cream shirt, matching tie and brown socks and shoes. Everything, right down to the shoes. As the night wore on seemingly one of the nurses just couldn't get over the outfit. He asked him what ward he was on. On being told he said, 'I thought I recognized Jimmy Laing's taste.'

I suppose that we didn't consider that we were actually stealing when we were manipulating the stores operation. We were playing a game where we made the rules, we were able to keep the patients well clothed and we had control over those who had control over us. There was actual stealing, in some cases by the staff. One nurse, who was eventually struck off the register after he was caught, would come into the kitchen store in our ward and help himself to cornflakes, cream crackers and anything else he could lay his hands on. You name it, he took it. If by chance you came in and found him he would just turn round and say, 'What the fucking hell do you want? I hope you're not looking to get anything for this, because you won't.' He would then take the items out of the back door and nip down to the car park and put them in the boot of his car.

One week he had been on relief duty and had finished on the Saturday night and left for his days off. The next charge nurse came on on the Sunday to find the larder cleaned out. He then turned on the patient who was in charge of the larder and demanded to know where the food was. The patient was on the edge of discharge and didn't want to get involved but the charge nurse told him that unless he spilled the beans, as it were, he would have him transferred to Medwin and his discharge would be in jeopardy. In the heat of the moment the patient poured out his story.

I hasten to add that the nurse in question had already been warned and had been told that he would be watched for any further instances of disappearing food while he was in charge. The charge nurse who had discovered the discrepancies immediately informed his superiors and an investigation began. He was then shunned by his colleagues for turning in his own kind. That was a pity as that charge nurse really was a very honest, fair man. A strict disciplinarian but never tyrannical. Straight down the line.

Two detectives from Lanark went to the guilty nurse's house to question him about the food which was missing from the State Hospital. When they went into the house they discovered an Aladdin's cave of goods. Seven pound tins of jam, twenty packets of cornflakes and more than fifty packets of cream crackers. He could have bought the cornflakes and the cream crackers but it was the jam which caught him out. The jam tins all had code numbers stamped on them and the company knew where they were sent to – in this case, the State Hospital. The policemen asked to see round the rest of the house and in one of the bedrooms was a top blanket on the bed; pink with the State Hospital name on it. He was advised by his union, the SPOA, that he should plead that he was a kleptomaniac and that he would put himself into Hartwood Hospital for treatment. This was certainly good advice as it would have meant that after treatment he would have had a job. He wouldn't have been a charge nurse again but he would have been kept on as a staff nurse. At least that would have been something. He refused the treatment and was struck off the register.

I learned this from the grapevine – the patients' one and the staff one. If you were in my position, wheeling and dealing on the black market, you kept your ear to the ground. There was always some member of staff who would tell you all the lurid details of cases concerning other staff, particularly if you got hold of a nurse who didn't like the nurse involved.

The thieving crew, like those involved in the brutality, were in the minority but they had a terrible influence over the others. A nurse would come in full of good intentions but he would be swayed by the others. I remember one young nurse who had just arrived and he and I were talking about instances of brutality. He said he abhorred the idea but he was quick to add, 'But mind, Jimmy, don't get me wrong, if I saw another nurse doing it I wouldn't witness against him.'

It was the code of conduct amongst them. I believe in unions but in this particular institution the SPOA was very, very powerful. They had to be listened to by the powers that be. If some progressive move was being made, for example a decision that Jimmy Laing was to be allowed out of the ward for an hour each day for a walk in the gardens, then somewhere along the line, someone might say, 'We can't have that.' There's nothing easier at Carstairs for a nursing officer than to pull 'security infringements' out of the air. It can sound impressive. 'Oh yes, he's got a point there. Patient Laing could act normally for a month going about his business. He then goes out into the gardens, enjoys his hour of parole but one day he climbs on to the chapel roof. What do we do then?' – knowing full well that Patient Laing won't do this. But the authorities have to listen to this and in most cases they won't take the risk of disagreeing with the nurse or the union. They had to rely on the staff and the last thing they wanted was any trouble.

While I believe that the selection of the staff and the training wasn't as it should have been, it wasn't helped that the basic staff and union attitude, in those days, was to keep the inmates contained, fed and calm and, it would follow, everything would be all right. This may be an attitude that would work on a group of identical people, but at Carstairs they weren't dealing with low-grade mental defectives, there were some highly intelligent patients in there and they needed to be treated as individuals.

Today, from what I hear, things are changing at Carstairs. The long-overdue rapport between staff and patients is coming into full play. They've reduced the numbers of patients and it's hoped that the numbers of nurses on duty at any one time will be increased to improve the treatment of patients. It is true that there are patients in Carstairs who have committed murder, rape and have molested children and it would be easy for outsiders to say that these people should be locked away without any form of treatment. After all, some would say, if we still had hanging many of them would have taken the drop. This is true but, equally, many of these murders are one-offs. The majority of them are very sad, tragic people. This is what the public do not know. They hear that someone has murdered his mother and they say, 'Oh that's hellish.' They don't know the ins and outs of the situation. I'm not saying there is any excuse for murder – that the end justifies the means – but you really have to be inside Carstairs and be with these people to see what they are going through. These people suffer a great deal – inwardly.

A patient can come into Carstairs and for the first few months he is coping with the place. In some cases he does not admit that he has committed the crime, such as the patient who butchered his daughters and left his wife a vegetable. He wouldn't even admit that they were dead at first. Then one day it suddenly comes to him that he has done this terrible crime. That's when the inward suffering begins. You can see it in their faces, punishing themselves day by day. That's where the staff must come in. If you have caring staff – and there were some – they would take notice of the patient's condition. On the other hand, there were those who just didn't know what to do and the patient would be left to suffer on his own.

That, in turn, is where the patients themselves used to come in. There was a limit to what you could do but you tried to help. But there's nothing more distressing than sitting with a patient who has just realized what an awful crime he has committed as he pours his heart and soul out to you. And you're thinking that, while the due process of law must be carried out, if this patient was released, the chances are he would never again commit such a crime.

You can see everything in the faces. The suffering, the remorse. This is where the different types of nurse come in. The good one will see a patient going downhill and do something about it in a caring way. The other type will resort to the 'liquid cosh' – drugs to stupefy the patient. I believe that the only way is to give the patient some understanding, love and care, in short the things which go hand in hand with 'real' nursing.

As time moved on at Carstairs psychoanalysis was introduced and this helped the patient who was going through traumas having realized his crime. Talking, talking all the time. Pouring it out and getting better. Too quick a recovery is not good though, it must be a slow process, week by week, session by session. Then comes the time when the patient is improving, taking an interest in what's going on round about him. Reading the papers again, playing football, going through the library shelves and talking to those in the ward with him. Suddenly some idiot of a nurse will come along and say, 'How are you today, Willie?'

'Oh fine, just fine thanks,' the patient would reply.

'A lot of shit you're giving us, isn't it, Willie? All this remorse. You're not sorry at all,' the nurse would then say and that could result in a setback for the patient. 'See, I told you so. Just an act,' the nurse would say.

That would seem a strange way for a psychiatriatric nurse to act but I use the term 'nurse' with reservation. It could be that a patient is having a shower, getting on fine. 'Come on you, are you no bloody finished there yet? Do you think you're the only one in the bloody ward!' a nurse would shout. Couldn't he have said, 'Come on, son, you've been in there long enough to wash yourself away, hurry up now.'

In my own case there was one occasion when I was rebelling against being locked up and generally I was on a downer. One particular nurse knew exactly how to deal with me and I appreciated it later. I think he knew that it would pay dividends. 'Now look, Laing, I'm bloody sick of this. I've bloody well bent over backwards for you. If I don't get any response from you you're out of this ward.' For me it certainly worked. That's what I mean; *he* knew his patients and how to deal with them. What a pity there weren't more of his kind.

One of the major improvements around that time was the introduction of the reporting procedure. It still had its drawbacks, but it was an improvement. In the beginning only one person was allowed to write the report, the charge nurse with the aid of his subordinates. The drawback in the system was that the charge nurse relied on the opinion of the nurses under him and there was no rhyme or reason behind those opinions. It is like the psychiatrists themselves. You'll never hear a psychiatrist saying, 'This patient is suffering from delusions of grandeur.' What he will say is, 'I am of the opinion that he suffers from delusions of grandeur.' There is a big difference in that. There can be a hundred different opinions amongst a hundred different people. As far as the treatment of patients is concerned I think that it would have been better to have had some set of standards by which a patient could be judged.

I could be standing by the window one day and something could go through my head and it would make me smile. I am sure everyone has done it at sometime or other, recalling maybe a little incident that had happened the day before. If you were seen doing that by a nurse it could be written up in your report that you were hallucinating. So you had to safeguard yourself from that. One incident that comes to mind involved an old chap from Dundee. Davy did everything very meticulously. Everything was done to perfection. One evening we were all queuing up for our two pints of lemonade, which was issued to us in case we wanted a drink during the night; Davy received his and I followed him up the stairs. As he turned the corner of our corridor, I was in Room 6 and he was in Room 3, he slipped and his two pints of lemonade went right over his head and all over me. Fortunately, he didn't hurt himself but he landed still holding the, by now empty, mugs. Well, I burst out laughing. He turned to me and asked, 'Was there something funny that happened?' That made things worse. I continued laughing. Of course it kept coming back to me and it made me continue to laugh. But I realized that my laughing could have been construed as hysterics. That night I rang the bell in my room and asked to see the night charge nurse. I related Davy's incident to him and that I had been laughing a lot and that when the thought of the incident came back to me it made me laugh and smile to myself. I just wanted him to be aware that I wasn't hallucinating if he were to see me doing it.

All this may seem a bit over the top to the casual observer but when the reporting procedures started the nurses were desperate to fill in the sheets with something and as their training, and the awareness of mental illness, wasn't necessarily of the best you had to be careful to cover yourself. Once something was on your file it never came off. It was important that they did write something. A good report would be something like 'James Laing: patient progressing well. Obedient, helpful, but tends to want more than his dues.' There was always a 'but', even in good reports. It would never have done for a patient to have a completely good report. It must be understood that if you are in Carstairs there must be 'something' wrong with you, according to the authorities.

A case in point was that of Jimmy, who had been accused of murdering a man. Jimmy went through the due process of law and ended up in Carstairs. But he didn't commit the crime. It was his brother-in-law that had murdered the man. Jimmy had taken the blame as his sister and brother-in-law had three children and he wanted to protect the family. He pleaded for fifteen years that he didn't do it but would never reveal the name of the person who had committed the crime. The psychiatrist at the time liked Jimmy and told him that the only way that he could do anything for him was for him to admit to the crime. Eventually Jimmy did this and after a time he was let out. During all this time his family visited him, twice a week. He must have gone through hell during those fifteen years. How easy it would have been for him to have his case re-opened by accusing his brother-in-law.

And all that time he refused. He had to wait until the system decided that he was ready to leave, after being compelled to admit that he was guilty. During those fifteen years his file would 'complement' his case. Things would be written down which would suit his case. It is very easy if someone is in Carstairs for a particular reason; everything he does or says can be attributed to that type of case.

One of the most shattering incidents that happened to me was later in my term at Carstairs when I acquired my own file. An enrolled nurse was leaving, he had been divorced and was getting married again. He came to me saying that he needed sheets and pillowcases, blankets and a duffel coat. I gave him these items, usually a few at a time. He'd have been caught if I had issued them all at once. Midway through the deal I told him that I wanted him to do something for me: I told him that I wanted my old file. By this time they had gone on to the new Kardex system and the old files were kept at the top of the cupboard in the charge nurse's office.

At first he refused so I told him that he was getting no more items. After all, I told him, 'It's you who wants the clothes and bedding, not me that's offering to sell them.' He eventually agreed. He duly presented me with it the night he was leaving. Twenty years of my life in one file. It was almost twelve inches thick. I was allowed upstairs to my store without supervision; as long as I was in the ward nobody bothered with me. I told the charge nurse that I was going to be very busy stocktaking so I didn't want to be disturbed and I put the file under some clothes in a basket and went to my store and locked myself in. I began to read what those in charge of me had written down for the past two decades: 'Self-deluded; manic-depressive; thinks staff are talking about him; hallucinates; is suicidal; hears voices.' And the most laughable bit: 'Patient steals a lot, always on the look-out for a bargain.' I would have liked them to elaborate and say, 'Takes two ounces of tobacco off staff when he sells them some State Hospital goods.' I thought, 'Christ, no wonder I'm here when I read all this.'

Without any power of redress, at that time, I was bloody upset about that file. But what could I do? Nothing. I decided that I had to get rid of it and so I got a galvanized pail of boiling water and pulped the lot and flushed it bit by bit down the toilet away out of my life. I often have wondered whether it would have been profitable for me to have kept it and in some devious way to have sent it out. I think not. At that particular period it wouldn't have been – maybe nowadays – but not then. I was in a quandary but I believe that I took the right steps.

In those days people, MPs and the like, didn't take an interest in a place like the CLD or Carstairs. You had no advocates in favour of reviewing the cases of the patients or inmates in institutions – unlike today. What I did do was to let it be known that I had stolen the file and destroyed it and then I spoke to the people who had written these terrible things about me. I'd go into the office at the right moment and say to a particular charge nurse,

'Why on earth did you say those things? You know they're not true.'

'Ach,' he would reply, 'you know we had to write those things, you're worrying about nothing.'

Nothing? I had done years in Carstairs, how many of them were as a consequence of my 'file'? I said to one of them, 'You know it's lucky that I'm not suicidal. If I had those tendencies I would certainly have done myself in after reading that file.' I just had to plod on hoping that things would improve. They did.

The new Kardex system which was brought in improved the quality of the reports. The doctors were no longer satisfied with: 'Patient went into the toilet and sat there for half an hour and then returned.' The doctors wanted to know why. The answer was usually quite simple: 'Patient constipated.' This demand for elaboration made the staff actually find out the reasons behind what was happening.

Some of the smarter nurses would catch on to this and one, in particular, would write his report with his medical dictionary beside him. The doctors would be very impressed. Others, though, just didn't have the savvy to catch on. One charge nurse always used the word 'dudgeon' when referring to a patient's condition. Dudgeon, in his mind, covered everything from upset through depression, elation, to violence. 'The patient was in high dudgeon today,' was his favourite expression. But Dr Neville wouldn't accept this type of report. He demanded, and got, elaboration. That's when the staff began to be a bit more careful. Also at this time all the nurses were allowed to write in the files and some of them began to get a bit carried away with themselves and were verging on spoiling the system operated by the old hands. I remember being told about one incident when a young auxiliary asked for my file one day. The charge nurse asked him why he wanted it. 'I've noticed that he's got too much tobacco as far as I'm concerned.'

'Away and don't be so daft,' the charge nurse told him. 'You'll learn eventually how he gets his tobacco.' The charge nurse told me all this later when he was up at my store. 'Silly bugger,' he said, 'he could have spoiled it for everyone.' This certainly elated me. I held no malice against the young nurse but it was good to feel that someone appreciated you, whatever the reason.

While things were improving on the reporting system that didn't mean life in Carstairs had suddenly become pleasant. There were still cases of victimization of the patients by the staff. If you weren't a 'popular' patient the staff would be able in their own way to get back at you if you had done something to annoy them. In the morning, at breakfast time, an 'unpopular' patient would ask for more porridge and the nurse would say there was none left. Then a 'popular' patient would ask and he would get some. That might seem an insignificant incident but it could have a devastating effect on certain patients. Some would take it quietly and others would blow up there and then and the staff would drag them away to their room, if they were lucky, and more likely to Medwin and out of their hair. But probably the most stupid thing happened when a patient asked for another roll one morning. '*Another* roll. Why do you want *another* roll?' asked the nurse. 'Because I'm hungry,' replied the patient.

Although these examples show the cruel side of the nursing staff – and they are only two out of many – there were some amusing incidents involving the staff. Sometimes, just for a bit of devilment, we'd be able to wind up the staff and get our own back on them. There was an old charge nurse who, every day, would bring two small pork pies in for his night-time snack. One day I stole one of these pies from his desk. He never said anything and the next day I stole another one. Again nothing was said so I continued to steal one every night he was on. It went on for almost two months. One day I said to him, 'God, Gordon, those pork pies look good. I wouldn't mind one of those.'

'Aye, sure,' he says, 'but, you know, someone has been stealing one of these pies every time I bring them in here and I'm buggered if I can find out who it is.'

'Well, Gordon, you know the score in here, patients don't talk about staff, but I think that it's that nurse over there.' I pointed out a nurse whom I knew to be leaving quite soon. Gordon then spluttered out, 'That's the bugger I thought it was all the time.' Good old Gordon. Some time before he retired I told him the truth. 'Ya bugger, ye,' he said. 'Do you want a pork pie then?' he added with a huge smile.

We had our practical jokers as well. George was one of the best. He had bought a false boil from a joke shop in Glasgow. It was very realistic. He turned up for the medical call and the charge nurse saw him. 'Oh my God, George, you come in first, that looks awful,' said the charge nurse. Out came the swabs, kidney-shaped dish and the lance. 'Oh no, no,' says George, 'I couldn't stand you lancing it. I'll do it myself.' And before the nurse could stop him he began to squeeze it, screaming in agony. The nurse grabbed him and made him stop. He started to wipe it with antiseptic and the boil fell off, much to the amusement of the other patients.

Our jokes weren't always at the expense of the nurses. Sometimes the patients got caught out as well.

We had a patient called Jackie who had been in for a long time. He used to run a fruit stall in Glasgow. He was fastidious in his cleanliness. One day Eddie, another patient, asked me if I'd like to take part in a little joke on Jackie. He asked me for a brand-new chamber pot out of my store. We took the pot and scalded it out with boiling water. Eddie then got a Mars bar and squeezed it out to look like faeces. The plan was to leave the pot near the sink so that when Jackie came up to wash his hands before supper he couldn't fail to see it. Eddie and I waited in the wings. When Jackie spotted the pot he let out a yell. 'Oh my God, that's disgusting.' Eddie and I rushed into the bathroom and asked what the problem was. 'Look at that,' said Jackie pointing at the pot. 'Oh I'll get rid of that,' said Eddie, and he picked up the supposed faeces and took a bite out of it. At first Jackie just stood and looked at Eddie in amazement. Then Eddie handed the pot to me and I picked up another piece and took a bite out of it. 'You're both bloody insane,' he screamed as he rushed out of the bathroom.

These were the things that made life a little more bearable in Carstairs. But all in all it was a hellish existence, particularly when you didn't think you should be there. Yes, there were times when I rebelled, times when I stepped out of line and times when I certainly misbehaved, but when you look at the way of life, together with the overall regime, it's hardly surprising.

9

Getting Out

At the beginning of 1972 Dr Loweg, one of the principal psychiatrists, began a programme which would lead to the release of some of the long-term patients.

Following a series of interviews and reports I arrived at my final interview. At the previous interviews I had refused to sit on the chair which was placed in the middle of the room in front of the interview board. I maintained that I wasn't an exhibit. I used to say, 'If you don't mind, gentlemen, I'll join you.' I suppose that this probably went against me but sometimes you have to stand up for your principles. On this occasion the chair was placed beside the interview board. I had arrived in the room with Dr Loweg who took a seat at the other end of the table. Now they say that psychiatrists cannot be fooled but believe me if you can tell them what they want to hear, sometimes they can.

'What do you think of your condition, Jimmy?' asked Dr Henderson. 'You seem to be making very good progress, taking the right steps, being helpful.'

I felt treated as though I was a three-year-old. 'And you really have been very co-operative during the past series of interviews. How has this come about?'

I pointed to Dr Loweg and said, 'Gentlemen, there is your answer. Without that man there I would be nowhere now. I would certainly not be sitting here in front of you being considered for release.'

You could almost hear Loweg purring with delight.

'We wish you well, Mr Laing,' said Dr Henderson. I went out and Loweg came rushing after me. 'We've made it, we've made it, Jimmy,' cried Loweg.

I thought, 'You silly bastard, if only you knew.' But I did the right thing and told him that I couldn't have done it without him. Before being let out I was taken for the day to Edinburgh. We would go in the car and the nurse would leave me at ten o'clock and arrange to meet me at five at the same place. Some days I would ask to be taken out to the old folks' home and I would sit all day talking to them.

While it had been almost twenty years since I had been in the outside world I didn't react in the way one might expect. I had made it my business to keep up to date with current events, reading papers, listening to the radio and watching television. I needed to do those things to keep my sanity. It was indeed great to be on the other side of the wire fence even for those few hours at a time. But as I didn't yet have my release papers I never allowed myself to accept that I would actually be released until the time came to leave Carstairs without having to return.

During this time Dr Loweg would call me into

his office and ask how I was getting on. 'Had a nice day out? Didn't fall off any pavements while you were out?' There were no pavements at Carstairs. I think he thought that I had never experienced pavements before. He would then say, 'See this bit of paper, James? You realize that I have to sign it before you get out? Without my signature it's worthless.' I thought, 'Eat humble pie, James, don't say what you'd like to say.' So I said to Dr Loweg, 'Oh you wouldn't do that to me, would you, Doctor?' You'd like to stand up and give him one on the chin or at least face him and say, 'OK, make your mind up. Either let me out or not, but stop teasing me.' But you can't. You have to sit there and take it. It's not like having a broken leg when you and the doctor know you're cured.

'I've really done so much for you, gone out on a limb, James, don't you agree?' he would say.

You had to reply, 'Yes, but you think it's worth it, don't you, Doctor?'

Then he would agree and say that he would let you know when he had decided to sign your papers.

You'd get up to leave saying, 'Thank you, Doctor, you're a real gentleman,' when you're really thinking to yourself that he's a real bastard. Humble pie can taste like eating shredded wheat without milk.

I went back to the ward and poured my heart out to one of the nurses whom I knew very well. 'Go on, thump him on the chin. If they do lock you up again I'll look after you.' It was very tempting but, no, I had to get out. The final release date arrived.

The social worker assigned to me, Clem McArthur, arrived to take me away from Carstairs.

The night before there had been quite a buzz in the ward from the patients. They genuinely felt happy for you, although some would be depressed about another patient getting out. They all knew that it was good for the hospital as it meant that the authorities were letting patients out and they might be next in line.

Some of the nurses congratulated me, others said, 'Oh, you'll be back.' One of my few regrets was that I was unable to personally pass on my 'business'. The staff themselves would decide who was 'trustworthy' enough to take over from me. My other regret was leaving my friends.

Clem and I got into his car outside the ward and we were off towards the main gate. We were just about through when there was a furious tooting of a car horn. I nearly died. It was Dr Loweg's car. I thought he was going to take me back. Clem said, 'Let's ignore him. He'll just be wanting to say goodbye and no doubt wanting you to thank him once again for all he's done for you. To hell with him.' We sped off.

What a delight finally to be out. There were conditions attached to my release. I was not allowed to associate with known criminals – I laughed at that, as if I wanted to – I had to report to my social worker and if I changed my address I had to inform my social worker before I did so.

We travelled to Stirling where Clem had organized my getting a job at the Golden Lion Hotel as a banqueting porter. I took to it right away. The manager had told the staff of my situation before I arrived. One thing began to bother me. During the day we'd all be working away setting the tables, hoovering and polishing and then in the evening the other porters would go downstairs and take the coats and show the guests up the stairs. There were, of course, gratuities paid out during this time and I never got any as I was told to stay upstairs out of the way. It wasn't anything to do with my background, more the case that they hadn't had a third porter for a long time and it would have meant sharing the tips three ways instead of two. I told the senior porter and he told me that it was because I hadn't been there long enough. So I made up my mind that I would make sure that I completed all my work in time for me to go downstairs and just put myself about. He wasn't likely to cause a scene in front of the guests. In one night I made almost a fiver.

But I decided that this wasn't the right way to go about things and while I knew that I could cope with a bit of aggravation from the other porters I didn't want to have it every time I saw them. So I decided to leave. I knew I was taking a risk not informing my social worker before I left but I thought I'd take the chance.

I headed for Edinburgh and once I had found lodgings I telephoned Clem. I told him I was doing OK and I explained the circumstances surrounding my departure from Stirling.

'Well, we won't tell Loweg,' said Clem. He really was a good man. One with common sense. Clem arranged better lodgings for me at a house run by the Church of Scotland. Their price included all meals and it was a very clean establishment. I began to look around for work. Without much difficulty I found one at the Greenlea old people's home where I worked as a porter. The shifts were split in three. One week on mail duty, one week on removing the incontinents' sheets to the laundry and the job I didn't take to – one week on death duty.

I had been working there for a few weeks when one day after taking the body of an old lady who had died that morning down to the mortuary I received a telephone call from the Matron to tell me that the family of the old lady were coming round to see the body. According to the Matron this was the first time they had been to see her for about six years. She asked me to go down to the mortuary and get the body out for the relatives. The Matron told me that she thought the old dear owned quite a lot of property in Queensferry Road, and to watch how the relatives would be grieving over their 'dearly departed relative'. I went downstairs and took out the body. I loosened the covering sheet, combed her hair and put some lipstick on her lips. It's strange to say but I got satisfaction out of it. Rather like when I looked after the old men in the CLD, it seemed to give her some dignity, even in death. I wanted her to look as beautiful as possible.

Sure enough the relatives arrived and did as the Matron had forecast. Tears everywhere. One of them did say that she looked beautiful. 'It's as though she's just sleeping.' While that made me happy I thought, 'My God, I've got to get out of here. I don't want to be dealing with dead bodies every third week for the rest of my life.' I told the other porters and left.

I had read an advertisement in the evening paper a few days earlier for a petrol pump attendant so I telephoned to see if the job was still vacant and was told to call in for an interview. I arrived at an office in Dalry Road and the secretary told me that Mr Mitchell would see me personally. While waiting to go in I wondered how I was going to handle the situation. I didn't want a third party coming in later and saying, 'You know he's from Carstairs?' so I thought that I'd come straight out and tell the truth. I went into the office and Mr Mitchell asked if I had ever done this type of work before. I told him that I hadn't but that I felt I could handle the job. Then I decided that I'd take the bull by the horns. 'There is something you should know. I'd prefer to tell you rather than you hear it from someone else. I have spent almost twenty years in Carstairs State Hospital.'

His reply was music to my ears. 'I'm not interested in where you've been. Do a good job of work for me, that's all I ask.'

I worked at the garage which dealt with all the Godfrey Davis rental cars. It was great fun and I fitted in well with everyone. I told Clem that I had moved jobs and he continued to make regular good reports about me to the Hospital. After working for Mitchell's for a while one of the Godfrey

Davis girls told me that there was a good job going at the Meadowbank Autopoint, just opposite Meadowbank Stadium. I went down to see them and they told me to start whenever I could. I went to Mr Mitchell and told him that I was getting a better job but out of loyalty to him I would stay until he found someone else. He was very good about it all and said that they would cope and for me to take the opportunity of the better job.

Again I told the manager of the petrol station all about myself and he said it didn't bother him as long as I worked well. One day, not long after I had been working there, I nearly died with fright. There in the forecourt was one of the senior Carstairs staff. It was a self-service station, and after he filled up his car he came into the shop to pay his bill. 'Well, well, James, and how are you getting on?' he said in a patronizing voice. 'How does it feel to be free?'

Quickly, I said, 'Yes, I'm so glad my divorce came through,' but I thought, 'You big-mouthed bugger. What if no-one knew about me? What questions they'd be asking now.' I told him what had happened since I left Carstairs, he said his goodbyes and left.

I enjoyed working at the Autopoint. I was accepted there as someone who did a good job and nobody bothered about my background. At last I felt that I was a genuine member of society, even though I was still under 'licence'. To keep myself busy in the evenings I took a voluntary job down at the old people's club in Portobello serving them tea, talking to them and playing dominoes. I really enjoyed being with them.

One evening I was chatting to another chap who helped out there. He was a policeman. We were talking about where each other stayed and he asked if I was interested in taking on a flat which belonged to an aunt who was moving to a retirement home. I went to have a look at it the next Saturday. It was just perfect. Situated on the prom at Portobello, it overlooked the swimming baths, had a lovely large sitting room, one bedroom, kitchen and bathroom, all fully furnished to a high standard. It cost eight pounds a week.

I had been in the flat only a short while when Clem telephoned to say that he wanted to bring down an official from St Andrew's House to see me. Clem had always said that he wanted me to be completely released right from the start and I knew that he was working on my behalf to that end. A few days later the official arrived at the flat with Clem. I had prepared a salad and had bought a bottle of wine. During the meal little was said. I told him where I was working and how I was getting on. I showed Clem round the flat and he seemed to be pleased with my progress and current situation. On their way out Clem whispered to me, 'I think we've done it.' I was elated. Out of the system at long last. It had taken a long time, thirty-three years, but at last I was going to be a free man.

My joy was to be short-lived. The next Monday the chap from the Scottish Office telephoned Dr Loweg at Carstairs and told him that he had seen me and that a discharge was now in order. To this day I believe that if Clem had even told Loweg that he had invited the Scottish Office official to see me and had added that it would be a good idea if Dr Loweg had joined them, then Dr Loweg, I'm sure, would have accepted that. Perhaps he felt he had been ignored.

Dr Loweg told Clem to arrange a meeting with me. He was hardly in the door when he told me, 'Do you know that I have the power to put you in my car and take you back to Carstairs? I won't, of course, but I'm just reminding you who's the boss around here.'

'I never thought you were anything else, Dr Loweg,' I replied. 'I hope that I haven't done anything to offend you, Doctor,' I pleaded. 'I thought you would be pleased to hear how well I was doing.'

This really stuck in my throat having to virtually crawl to him. Before leaving he tore a strip off Clem for daring to interfere with the case of one of *his* patients. Then he turned to me and said, 'Goodbye, James, and don't forget to take a look in the mirror now and again.' I never worked out what that meant. I was frightened. Of course he could take me back to Carstairs whenever he wished. All he had to say was, 'I think that James needs a rest and should come back to the Hospital for a time.' If that had happened I would never have been let out again.

I decided that I had to get away even though there were risks involved. I was supposed to tell Clem about any change of job or address but I felt that that would put a great deal of responsibility on to him and I didn't want that.

I aimed to get as far away as possible. I packed my bags, went and saw the landlord to settle my rent, explained my predicament to the manager at the petrol station, collected my savings from the bank and headed off to Cornwall. That was the furthest place I could think of. I was very upset to leave my lovely flat. Things had been going so well. Now my world had collapsed again.

I eventually arrived in Bodmin after a long journey by train and bus. I got a room in a small inn in the town. I had about two hundred pounds which I had saved up over the months at the garage. I had worked a lot of overtime, particularly at the weekend, so the money had mounted up. Even so, I went to the Social Security office and told them that I was down in Cornwall looking for work but that I had no money. In those days they didn't bother to check and they gave me a Giro cheque which would keep me going until I got a job. I decided to find cheaper lodgings. I asked around and was directed to a large Victorian house set in its own grounds. It was owned by a retired Naval Commander and his wife. He was a tall elegant-looking gentleman. His wife dealt with letting the rooms. She took me upstairs to a lounge which was for the use of the paying guests. This room was down at the end of a large hall which had five bedrooms leading off it. Each bedroom was well decorated and meticulously clean. There was a kettle and teapot, cups and saucers and each room had a small fridge. The weekly rental included breakfast.

After we had looked around the house the lady

turned to me and said that I could have one of the rooms. 'You'll be wondering why I made such a quick decision. You have clean shoes,' she told me.

I checked out of the inn and took my belongings round to my new lodgings and began to look for work. A few days later I was standing outside the court in Bodmin just looking around when I saw a blue Austin pulling up opposite me. There sitting in the car was a nurse from Carstairs. I thought, 'My God, he's duty bound to say that he's seen me.' I was to find out later that it wasn't him at all; that particular nurse couldn't drive. I panicked, rushed back to my lodgings, made up an excuse to the landlady that I had to return to Scotland urgently as my sister was ill, paid my bill and left.

All the time I was looking over my shoulder. I caught a bus from Bodmin to Exeter and then on to Glasgow via Birmingham. From there I went to Perth and on to Inverness. My eventual destination was my niece's house in Lybster near Wick. I arrived in Inverness about six o'clock in the evening. I had nowhere to go and although I still had some money in the bank, they were all closed and I had almost spent what I had had on me when I left Bodmin.

I saw this chap across the bus station and I walked over to where he was sitting and we began to chat. I knew that he was, like me, a homosexual. There's a sexual chemistry between homosexuals. You don't have to say 'I'm gay' or even make certain movements. It is something you detect without words being spoken. Homosexuals recognize other homosexuals. It's just there. We went off for a walk down the Fort William Road. We stopped at an embankment out of sight of the road. I suppose it seems like an excuse to say that I was lonely and depressed with all the goings on that had happened to me over the past few days but here I was with someone who was lending a sympathetic ear and that meant a lot. We lay down on the grassy embankment and had sexual satisfaction. Then he wanted to leave but I wanted him to stay with me for a while. I felt hurt and abused that he just wanted me as a sexual object. I set about attacking him and I hit him with a branch. His head began to bleed profusely. I thought, 'Oh my God, I've done it this time.'

There was a little stream nearby and I got my handkerchief and began to bathe his head. I told him that I would take him to the main road and try to find someone to help him. A little up the road I saw a farm and went up the lane to ask for help. I rang the bell but all we got was a barking dog. By now it was almost midnight. I decided that we should go back to the main road to see if I could get him a lift back to Inverness and to hospital. I think that we must have looked a strange sight; me holding up this person who's still bleeding and trying to flag down a car. No wonder no-one stopped.

We decided that it would be best if we split up and each tried to get a lift separately. The bleeding had almost stopped and his idea seemed to be the better. I was also glad to get away from the situation as I knew that if he went to a hospital questions would be asked and I would be involved. I went back towards Inverness and went into the grounds of Craig Dunain Hospital where I sat in a gardener's hut until morning. I spent the night thinking, asking myself where it had all gone wrong. Yes, I could find a million excuses but none of them acceptable in the cold light of dawn. I was glad that the chap seemed to be all right but I was very frightened.

In the morning I caught a bus to Golspie, which was as far as I could get on the money I had left. From Golspie I got a lift by lorry into Wick. The driver pointed out the road to Lybster and said that I'd soon get a lift. By now it was getting on for evening. I began walking towards Lybster when a car stopped and offered me a lift. I told him that I was going to see my niece whom I had never seen in my life before. Fortunately he never asked me to elaborate on my situation. When we arrived in Lybster we stopped at the Post Office to ask for directions. I found out that her house was about five minutes' walk away so I made to say goodbye to the driver but he insisted that he would drive me there. Call it fate, bad luck or coincidence, I was to discover later that my driver was a plain-clothes policeman. Even when he was peering out of the car at the house number it never occurred to me that he was being anything other than helpful. I arrived at the address and Judith came to the door. 'I'm Uncle Jimmy,' I said.

'You'd better come in then,' she replied.

While I had never met her or her husband Robert,

they knew all about me. Judith's mother was my sister May who lived in Orkney and to whom I had been sent many years previously on that ill-fated trip. Robert sat me down and gave me a stiffener of a whisky. 'Are you in trouble?' he asked. I told him that I didn't want to involve him and the family and it was better that nothing was said. We sat down to a meal which, as I had not eaten for the past two days, tasted delicious.

About seven o'clock that evening there was a knock at the door. Robert answered it and I heard a voice asking, 'Do you have a Mr James Laing here?' Robert asked the person what he wanted and the voice said, 'Do you think that he might come down to the police station at Wick to answer a few questions?' I got up and went to the door and said, 'It's all right, Robert, I know what it's about. I'll come with you, officer.' The policeman standing in front of me was an old constable. He said to me, 'You're not going to give me any trouble are you, son?' Robert said he would come down with me and I think the constable breathed a sigh of relief.

The police station in Wick was a very small one and while they had cells they allowed me to sit in the mess room while they waited for two detectives to come up from Inverness. I told Robert that I would be all right and that he should go home. While I was sitting there on my own I had time to reflect on my life since my flight from Edinburgh two weeks previously. What a disaster I had made of it. Perhaps I shouldn't have run away from Edinburgh in the first place but I was scared that

Dr Loweg would have taken me back to Carstairs. It's easy to say, with hindsight, particularly after all that had happened, that I should have stayed and if Dr Loweg had tried to take me back I could have appealed to Clem and the Scottish Office official to stop him. But you have to remember that even then, in 1973, there was no redress or appeal procedure. When you have lived in a system that totally controls your life you are not able to think rationally when you feel threatened by that system.

The two detectives arrived just after three in the morning. The younger one said to me, 'Right, Jimmy, I've got handcuffs here if they're needed. Do you think they're needed?' I replied that there was no need and that I wouldn't cause any trouble. 'Good,' he said. 'I'm absolutely bushed and I'd like to grab some sleep on the way back.' We left Wick and they both took it in turns to drive while the other had a sleep in the back.

On the way I asked the younger one how they had tracked me down. He told me that the chap I had been with had reached the hospital and had given my name and a description to the police who had circulated it round the country. When the details arrived at Wick they had been seen by the detective who had given me the lift and he was able to take them straight to my niece's door. What a coincidence that had been.

We arrived at Inverness police station where I was told that the chap was now out of hospital and was all right. From there I was taken to the court in the Castle where I was charged with attempted murder. I was remanded in custody and sent to Porterfield Prison. In the prison I was asked if I wanted to see Dr Loweg who had come up from Carstairs. I refused. I wanted to be tried as a normal human being not as an 'ex-Carstairs' patient. I knew that if I was found guilty whatever the prison sentence it would be less than the time they would keep me in Carstairs. If I was returned to Carstairs I would have to start all over again. I would have let down the system and that would look very bad on their records.

I was remanded in Porterfield for almost three months and during the last week before my trial I was allowed the freedom of the prison. My door was only locked at night. Two days before my trial, which was to be Lord Grieve's first High Court trial, I decided to write to him to explain my case. I wrote that I was guilty as charged although there were, I believed, extenuating circumstances, but I wished to be tried as a normal person and sentenced accordingly rather than be tried as a former psychiatric patient. Whether or not it would have done any good wasn't helped by the fact that my lawyer handed the letter to the judge after the trial. My trial in front of Lord Grieve was a very quick affair. In court were two psychiatrists, Dr Whittet and Dr Trent, who had spent the previous weeks examining me, or so they claimed, to find that I needed further psychiatric care.

The sentence was that I should be returned to Carstairs. When he passed sentence his words took me back all those years to my earliest days in mental institutions. 'Am I to understand that when he goes back it will be for a short time, until he's well again?' asked Lord Grieve. 'Oh yes,' replied the psychiatrists.

I asked if I could make a statement. I stood up and bowed to the judge and said, 'Unknowingly, My Lord, you have made a grave mistake. Through no fault of your own you are signing my death-warrant in sending me back to Carstairs.'

I was put into the custody of a psychiatric nurse from Craig Dunain Hospital in Inverness. He was very sympathetic. He had sat in court during the trial and when we left the court he said to me, 'Bugger the lot of them. Let's go and have some lunch before you have to come back.' We went to a hotel and had mince and potatoes. It was like the condemned man having his last meal before the drop.

10

Return to the System

We arrived back at Carstairs around nine o'clock that night. On the journey from Inverness everything had been racing through my mind. Fear, trepidation, annoyance at letting myself get into such a situation. It was the end, I thought. Would I ever again be free or was the period of my few months out the last time I would ever be allowed to live a life of my own? I was returning to the system that I hated. A system which didn't allow you to think for yourself. I would be put right back at the bottom of the pile. I had to start all over again.

Thirty years previously I had been sent to Baldovan. It had only been 'for a little while'. At Murthly again there was no limit of time. Now after years at Gartloch, the Criminal Lunatic Department and Carstairs itself, I was returning to the system where time would not exist. I would have to face the nurses who would tell me, 'I knew you would be back'. I would face those who would delight in tormenting me over my failures; those who would even delight in telling me that I would probably never be allowed out again. And I would have to face Dr Loweg, who, I knew, would take my case as a slight on his professionalism.

The morning after my arrival the nurse on duty came to my bed and said, 'Your friend's here, Jimmy.' Dr Loweg had arrived. He appeared at the door of the ward, came in and sat on my bed. 'Young man,' he said, 'last night I wept for you. I was really weeping.'

I was cornered. Right of reply wasn't in his book. 'I'm going to ignore you for a few weeks,' he said. 'I'll come back then and you're going to tell me all about what happened to you and why. I am also not going to leave you here in the hospital wing, that's not necessary. Sadly I'll have to send you back to Medwin. I have to make it appear that I am not being lenient with you.'

All the time his intention was to let me know that I was back and I was totally under his control. I was sent to Medwin and did not see Dr Loweg for four weeks. Those first few weeks were hellish. I was surrounded by the lowest level of patients – men who spent the day shuffling around drugged up to the eyeballs.

Around this time, autumn 1973, the courts began to send more people to Carstairs. It gave *them* a fright to be there. This meant that the State Hospital was filling up and wards such as Medwin were the favourite place to put the new arrivals. When Dr Loweg arrived to see me the charge nurse told him that I had been a model patient and that if I wasn't moved out he was prepared to go to the authorities to have me moved. Reluctantly Dr Loweg agreed. I was sent back to Forth ward and Dr Loweg began visiting me to, as he put it, 'allow me to cleanse my soul of what has happened'. I decided in the initial stages that I wasn't going to explain the homosexual side of my case. Psychiatrists can read sex into everything. It has been known for a psychiatrist to ask a patient who hadn't paid his fare on a bus if that gave him 'a sexual thrill.'

Of course, Dr Loweg knew all about my case from the court and prison records and it was only a matter of time before I told him everything. It wasn't that I wanted to hold anything back but he had worked out his own reasons for my return before he even spoke to me and I wanted to tell him what had happened in my own way and not under the pressure of his questioning which was only leading to the answers which he wanted to hear. It was better to agree with him and accept everything he said: if I was to have any hope of ever getting out again I had to play Dr Loweg's game.

Many nights I would lie awake thinking about the time I had spent outside. I was confident that if I had the chance again I would make it. It's a known fact that the second time you're out of Carstairs it is easier to make it providing your case isn't too serious. By Christmas 1973 I was back in my store job more or less taking over from where I had left off. I had had to eat humble pie to get that position back but this time it was a little less 'dry' than before.

By the spring of 1974 I was really back into the black market economy. I was doing well.

I had been 'promoted' within the ward by the charge nurse without the senior staff's instructions and they didn't like that, with the result that I was transferred to another ward, where they already had a storeman and I would just be another patient like the rest. Unfortunately the charge nurse there and I had a mutual dislike for each other. Before I left Forth the charge nurse there, Ronnie MacVicar, had told me that one of the nurses in my new ward hated my guts. As far as I was concerned this nurse, whom we'll call Smith for now, had the wrong attitude towards myself and the other patients and I had told him so on many occasions. Before I had got out in 1972 I had also mentioned his conduct to one of the psychiatrists and the report had got back to him. But he had his revenge on me. He had another nurse write up a report about me alleging a host of mistruths and lies and he had signed it. I often wondered if Dr Loweg knew about this and, indeed, about the subsequent relationship.

I spent the first month trying to avoid Smith but it was very difficult. I would keep myself to myself as much as possible. Anything that I was asked to do I did right away without any comment. Then Smith went on holiday for three weeks and Willie Jamieson took over. He and I had always had a good relationship and he told Dr Loweg that he was going to promote me to kitchen man, the person that looked after the kitchen on a day-to-day basis, ordered the food necessary for the snacks and generally kept the place tidy.

Dr Loweg came in one day and asked for a cup of coffee. 'By gosh, the staff like you, don't they, James?' he said. 'I wonder why?'

I replied, 'Well, Mr Burnside says I'm a model patient, Doctor.'

'Well, I'll be keeping a check on your progress, James, and I'll be asking Mr Smith what he thinks when he returns,' said Dr Loweg as if to remind me that things could be changed with one stroke of the pen.

Smith returned from holiday and there was an air of tension immediately. He wanted to remove me from the kitchen but I had other ideas. Smith had had a habit of coming into the kitchen after the weekly supplies had been delivered. These supplies were ordered by the kitchen man and included biscuits, cheese, apples and other fruit, tea, sugar, salt and vinegar and lemonade. Smith, it seemed, would, in the past, come in and help himself to some of the supplies. One night I had obtained extra apples and I took them into the day room and offered them to the patients. Smith jumped up and said, 'I want those apples. I always take them to an old man in Carnwath.' I knew he was lying. I told him that he couldn't do that and that they were the patients' apples and that I had to share them out. He went out and slammed the door. That left a six-mile gap between us, which widened further when another incident occurred in the kitchen.

I was always meticulous in my preparation of

the food and one day Smith arrived in the kitchen and began to take some of the food out of the containers with his hands. I told him to stop it and at least get a spoon. Again he went out and slammed the door.

A few days later I was in the day room and a patient, Jimmy Doyle, asked me if Smith was still taking his cut from the provision on a Thursday. 'Not that I know of,' I replied, 'certainly not while I was there.' Jimmy then told me that he used to come in and take half a dozen packets of biscuits and a lump of cheese that he claimed he was taking to the 'old man' in Carnwath. One of the patients, who was an admirer of Smith, now went and told him that he was being accused of stealing. Smith came bursting into my room later that afternoon and began shouting at me. 'You're accusing me of stealing!' he yelled.

'Not me,' I replied. 'You've got it all wrong. You did it when Jimmy Doyle was in the kitchen. He asked me if you were still taking the biscuits and the cheese. Ask Jimmy Doyle.' I went out and shouted for Doyle and hardly were the words out of my mouth than Doyle admitted that he had told me. At that Smith stormed out of the room and I followed him yelling that he could stuff the kitchen job and he could find another skivvy.

While I was glad that I didn't have to deal directly with Smith the argument upset me a great deal and I decided that I would have to find something else to take up my time. I made an appointment with Dr Loweg and while it stuck in my throat to ask him I told him that I felt that our interviews were helping me a great deal and did he think that a spell in the occupational therapy unit would be beneficial for me? He beamed at me when I told him and said, 'James, my boy, I also think that you're doing well and certainly a period in occupational therapy would do you the world of good.' How you can get your own way when you play their games! Unfortunately the incidents with Smith had been reported to Dr Radcliffe and as I wasn't able to put my side of the story on the file I was once again cast as the villain. But at least I was out of his way during the day and that was a relief.

One evening, a few months later, while Smith was eating his tea in the day room watching the television, another patient came to me to tell me that Smith's coat was stuffed full of items belonging to the hospital. He said to me, 'Look, I'll watch out for you. You know that he always sits and watches *Scotland Today* on STV every evening. You can go and empty them and I'll put them in my locker.' I went over to his coat which had poachers' pockets in it. 'How apt,' I thought. I searched through his pockets and found handkerchiefs, socks, soap, shoelaces and even a vest. I put them all in a plastic bag and put them in the other patient's locker. I didn't know until the next day that one of the nurses knew what was happening and had stayed out of the way. He told me what happened the next day. Seemingly Smith had come to collect his coat and when he found that it didn't weigh as much as he thought it should his face fell and he frantically went through his pockets. Of course he couldn't say that anything was missing and even when he found out what had happened at a later date he could hardly accuse me of stealing his property when he had stolen it in the first place. Very quickly the word went round the hospital that I had sorted him out. I had got some revenge over the report he had written about me. But the best was yet to come. A few months later I was transferred back to Forth ward and one evening Smith appeared to work some overtime. He said to me, 'Well, Jimmy, how are you keeping these days?'

'I'm doing very well, Mr Smith,' I replied, 'but, more to the point, how can you sleep at night?'

At this point one of the other nurses said, 'Och, come on, Jimmy, that's all over and done with now. Let bygones be bygones.'

I turned to Smith and said, 'Are you aware of the damage you did to me over that report you wrote about me? Everyone knows you were so full of hate that you couldn't write a fair assessment and just wrote a load of lies about me.' His face turned purple with rage and embarrassment but before he could say anything the other nurse led him away and I was sent to the day room.

Later that night I spoke to the other nurse and told him that although I wasn't in charge of the kitchen, if I saw Smith coming out of the kitchen with a sandwich in his hand I would report him for theft of hospital property. He fell into my trap. It may not be the correct way to behave but inside Carstairs when you can you fight fire with fire.

Sure enough Smith appeared out of the kitchen with two cheese sandwiches.

'That's hospital food you're eating,' I told him. 'Food for us patients. You'd better put it back or I'll charge you with theft.' I meant it. 'I'll get the police in and tell them that you are stealing hospital food.'

The other nurse tried to intervene and told me that that was enough and to stop it. But I had to get my revenge. That bastard had put years on my stay at Carstairs with his reports. When I read them I wept, particularly over the phrase, 'The patients shun him.' That bit hurt most. Smith put the bread back and if looks could kill I'd be dead by now. I didn't enjoy it one bit but it had to be done. The only satisfaction I got was later that night when I was handing in my store keys and I said goodnight to the other nurse on duty.

'Aye, you'd better get to your bed,' he said. 'You've had a full day of it today, you bugger, haven't you?'

I replied, 'It was quite good, wasn't it? Imagine me talking to a charge nurse like that. You'll have to report it, I suppose.'

We went upstairs and Smith was standing outside my room. I turned to the other nurse and asked him if he would lock my door as I didn't want anything more to do with Smith that night. 'Good night, Smith,' I said and as the lock was turned I heard him kick the door. Not a word was reported. I lay on my bed and thought back over the day. I hadn't enjoyed doing what I did but I had to do it. Even though what I had done had been trivial compared to what he had done to me and other patients over the years, I had had to repay him in kind to get some form of revenge.

11

The Incident

The year 1976 marked a horrendous tragedy at Carstairs. Two patients murdered another patient and a nurse, broke out of the Hospital, murdered a policeman and left another policeman paralysed. In Carstairs it became known euphemistically as the Incident. The two patients who committed the atrocities were Tom McCulloch and Robert Mone.

These were two of Dr Loweg's patients. He had plans to get them out together once he considered them 'cured'. What he did not realize, despite his years of experience, was that Mone was a psychopath. McCulloch and Mone were an unlikely pairing. McCulloch was well educated and came from a good family. Mone, on the other hand, was completely different. He certainly had a murderous background. He had been sent to Carstairs for shooting a schoolmaster in Dundee where he also injured some of the pupils in the school. Even the way he walked was sleekit. If you caught him off guard you could see the killer instinct in his eyes.

But then again he could go and pick up a bird with a broken wing and nurse it back to health. McCulloch and Mone had conned their way into running the hospital magazine as editor and printer. At the same time they were both working in the joinery workshop of the occupational therapy unit. They were very willing workers but it was all a cover for their heinous plans.

I always prided myself in being able to anticipate the unexpected; I had learned it over the years as a form of self-protection – but they were very good at concealing their objectives and I did not realize what was going on. During the summer months previous to the Incident occurring I was working in my store in Forth ward. It was upstairs beside the fire-escape. When the weather was warm the door would be left open, although the barred door was still closed, and I used to sit and look out over the hospital grounds. I saw the two of them day after day. The procedure was always the same. Mone would leave Clyde ward and McCulloch would leave Tweed ward, next to Clyde, at the same time. McCulloch always carried a black wooden attaché-case. They would walk together towards an old air-raid shelter which was a bicycle shed. Later it was found out that they had a box there where they were hiding some of the items they would use in the escape.

On the night of the Incident there was to be a rehearsal of a play being put on by the patients. Again Mone and McCulloch were involved. They had devised the play, written and produced it. The characters included patients dressed up in nurses' outdoor uniforms. They had everything worked out. Their plan was to use the uniforms to disguise themselves while they were making their escape. They had told two of the patients involved in the play that the rehearsal was cancelled but had not told the nurse in charge of the unit. He was Neil McLelland, a likeable person in every way and one of the few who wanted all patients to improve themselves while they were in Carstairs. That was to be his downfall. He was completely taken in by this pair. The night in question he collected Mone and McCulloch and another patient named Ian Simpson who had got in tow with the other two. Simpson had been sent to Carstairs after he had been found guilty of murdering three foreign hikers in the Inverness area. McLelland made a cardinal error that night and he paid with his life. The general rule at Carstairs is that there must be two staff with each patient if they are being moved at night, for whatever reason. McLelland broke that rule. He picked up Simpson, first, then Mone and finally McCulloch to take them to the supposed rehearsal of the play. When they arrived at the rehearsal room they found that there was a female recreation officer there, Mary Hamilton. They started an argument with her and Neil told her to go down to the recreation hall and that he would be all right on his own with them. Then they committed their terrible deed.

The first any of us knew about it was when a nurse came out of his office, his face white as a sheet.

'Everybody upstairs to bed, right now,' he said. This was an hour and half before our bedtime. I asked him what was the matter. 'Listen to your radio,' he said.

Just as we got into our rooms the sirens went off. There had been a break-out. It wasn't as simple as that. Later the full horror of that night came out. Mone and McCulloch had not only escaped but had murdered McLelland and Simpson. What transpired was that Simpson had been murdered sitting at McLelland's desk. They had cut off his ears and slit his throat. This gave rise to the idea that while he had been happy to go along with the escape, at the last moment he was going to become a hero and dial the emergency number to stop it and then he would get the credit and presumably be let out as a reward. I and many others at Carstairs who knew him felt that there could be some truth in that theory. McLelland was hacked to death about six feet away from his desk. They found the bloody handprints on the wall where he had slid down to the floor.

Mone and McCulloch murdered both of them with the knives and axes they made when they were working in the occupational therapy unit while they were being so 'willing' to please everyone. They then colllected a rope-ladder, which they had made, from the box at the back of the bicycle shed and went over the wire fence at the Carnwath Road. Mone lay down in the road when they heard a car coming and by pure coincidence it was the local police patrol. One got out to investigate the supposed problem and he was attacked and killed.

The knife that Mone used is in the black museum at Carstairs. It was over a foot long, honed to razor-sharpness. They then set about the other policeman and left him for dead. He survived but as a cripple.

It was then, about an hour and a half after the murders had happened, that the alarms went off. Later at the inquiry held into the Incident great stress was placed on the delay. Apparently the murders were discovered only by accident when a nurse who was out in the grounds for some reason happened to pass the room where the murders had taken place, saw the trail of blood and set off the alarms.

By this time we were all locked in our rooms but as I had a high-frequency radio I was able to tune in to the police channels. What happened next was that Mone and McCulloch, dressed in nurses' outdoor uniforms, took the police car towards Biggar. There they went to a farmhouse and terrorized the residents who handed over their car to them. By this time the police were on to them and they chased them to Carlisle where they were finally forced off the road and caught.

Although I was listening to the radio I didn't know at that stage that they had committed the murders. I thought that they had just escaped. It was the next day that I was told what had happened. I was shaken by the news of Neil's death. I had spoken to him at three o'clock that afternoon and he had been telling me that he was preparing things for Christmas and that we must talk about the presents that were going to be bought for the patients. I said to him that he should go into one big store in Glasgow and get the lot. Mary Hamilton had also been there and she suggested that he buy the decorations there as well. He said to me, 'I'm going to tell Bill Watt', the departmental charge nurse, 'that I need you to help out with the Christmas things. Better the devil you know than the devil you don't know.' He said his goodbyes and left me some newspapers and some tobacco. As I walked out of the room there was Mone sitting sorting out some magazines. It never occurred to me that anything was wrong. But how prophetic Neil's words were. The devil he didn't know was Mone.

The next day blame was being apportioned all over the place but I knew, as did everyone else, that it had been Neil's fault. He should never have taken three patients out on his own. Everything you touched seemed to smell of death that day.

The SPOA immediately stepped into the breach and took immediate action which involved locking out the doctors. They laid the blame squarely on the doctors' shoulders. The regime in the wards was very strictly controlled by the nurses. As far as they were concerned the Incident merely confirmed their idea that the only way to control mental patients such as those at Carstairs was containment. The doctors turned up each morning at the hospital gates but were turned away. They even turned up some mornings with placards and, naturally, the press and television crews surrounded the place.

The situation began to resolve itself after Professor McCrae had a letter drafted and sent out to all the nurses accusing them of neglecting the patients – we hadn't seen a doctor for over a week and some of the patients were getting into a terrible state. When a patient, particularly the lower grades, is in a mental hospital, he requires a regular lifestyle. It's part of the treatment. It's essential that this type of lifestyle is maintained. Anything that disrupts it can only do damage. This was the case at Carstairs following the Incident.

Eventually the doctors were let back in. I remember seeing Dr Loweg walking about the grounds. He looked completely stunned. I think that he took much of the blame on his own shoulders. He was the one who considered that Mone and McCulloch were progressing well. He was the one who sanctioned their treatment and he was the one who could have been killed instead of Neil McLelland. It emerged after the Incident that their original plan was to kill Dr Loweg when he took them out for the day to Biggar. Fortunately for the doctor, that trip had been cancelled.

During the inquiry which followed it was revealed that the police had found a veritable arsenal of weapons in secret compartments in the occupational therapy workshops: knives honed down to a fine point, chains and coshes all made by Mone and McCulloch while they were working on coffee tables and the like. One of the problems was that the nurse in charge of the workshops was in a booth inside the workshops from where he issued the tools. The problem was that the nurse had a restricted view of the workshop, and therefore couldn't see exactly what the patients were up to unless he came out of the booth and by that time Mone and McCulloch would see him coming and hide their weapons. There was also a slackness in the checking of the tools in and out. If, say, a chisel went missing there didn't seem to be much of a fuss over it. After the Incident all tools were checked in and out and each tool had its own place on the board in the booth and if any was missing the whole place was checked until it was found – a case of bolting the stable door after the horse had run away.

I suppose it would be very easy to blame the nurses who were on duty in the workshops but their attitude was very positive in those days. They were instructed what to do and they carried out their duties, although it has to be said that if you are a psychiatric nurse then you should always be on your guard. But when you consider the type of people that Mone and McCulloch were then probably even the most aware nurse would have been conned. Even if the murders had never been committed though, there should have been some set-up which would have ensured the checking of tools.

While Dr Loweg took some of the blame and Neil McLelland certainly became the whipping boy, another nurse took considerable treatment after the Incident. Neil's son blamed the Chief Nursing Officer, Tom Oswald, for his father's death and for almost two months would put an envelope through Tom's letterbox at home with a message inside which said, 'You Murdering Bastard'. I can still see Tom walking up towards our ward. He was looking for comfort during these times. Fortunately we had a very sensible nurse on duty, Jimmy Beveridge, and he spent many hours with Tom talking to him and consoling him.

As far as the overall attitude of the staff towards the patients was concerned there was a great deal of apprehension. The murders had happened out of the wards but could it happen at ward level? One good thing that did happen was that the goading by the nurses seemed to calm down a bit. They were so busy in the security sense, that they didn't have time.

About six months after the Incident things began to be a bit more relaxed but only at ward level. Ground parole, whereby the trusted patients were allowed to move about the ground with only cursory supervision, had been stopped as soon as the Incident had happened and the movement of patients was strictly controlled. Discharges and transfers were also put back. Staff at Woodlea Hospital, for instance, would say, 'We're certainly not having anyone from Carstairs.' We were all tarred with the same brush.

During this six-month period we had had the internal inquiry. It was a dress rehearsal for the public inquiry which was to follow but it really was the time for the staff, who by now had the authorities in a vice-like grip, to exert their power and ensure that all their fears and comments would be brought out. They said that they were unhappy that the doctors did not consult them over which patients should have ground parole and which should not. They had a point there when you consider that Dr Loweg would come into a ward and say that he had decided that James Laing should have ground parole. Probably it would have been better all round for him to suggest that James Laing was ready for ground parole and then ask what the charge nurse thought. I suppose when you consider the combination of the quality of the staff and the doctors' attitude towards them it wasn't difficult to understand why they weren't asked for their views. But it all added up to a further breakdown of relationships between staff and doctors and we patients were in the middle of all this.

When it came to the public inquiry the Chairman and the Board of Management were shown up in a very bad light. They got a terrible going over at the inquiry. Yes, they were credited with discussing some things that were for the patients' own good such as having new curtains in the wards or having cushions for the wooden chairs but they didn't really know what went on inside the Hospital and they should have. It was just a nice day out for them; lunch and pat the people on the head once a month.

But why had it all happened? It wasn't just because Mone and McCulloch were clever enough to con the system. Prior to the Incident progressive moves had been instituted but I believe they were brought in too fast. We were asked to a meeting in the ward while these measures were in force and I piped up that I felt that we already had our top storey built and yet we hadn't laid the foundations properly. That was my feeling about it. Progress is important but slowly, not in the leaps and bounds which we were experiencing.

There was no continuity, no rapport. On the contrary, there was a great deal of discontent in the hospital principally arising from the lack of consultation between staff and doctors. Dr Loweg, for example, was a strong character. His intentions were good but his methods were wrong. He would have had a lot more co-operation from the staff if he had taken them into his confidence but that wasn't his way. He would not communicate with them.

It is true that one of the problems Carstairs faces is that they are dealing with some of the lowest levels of mental patients. The psychotic criminal. But there is still a great deal of pressure on the psychiatrist to prove that these people can be cured. What Dr Loweg was doing was trying to show that the system could cure these people.

It has to be remembered that in such an environment it could be like a powder keg some days. For months and even years it could be calm but there's always the chance that something could happen. The Incident had proved that. But another cause could be apathy. An apathetic approach by the staff means that the whole regime suffers. 'Let's leave it to the doctors', became the phrase most heard in the wards.

There should have been consultation. Even if it began as a pretence, later something would have come out of it, I'm sure. In Dr Loweg's case his pomposity didn't endear him to the staff. He could have changed things which would have helped all round.

While it was true that the quality of the staff was less than desired, doctors such as Loweg could have raised staffing standards. Why, for example, didn't he get them together, explain what he was trying to do with a patient, explain the patient's background and circumstances? The staff would have understood him more and they would have understood the patient which surely would have led to a better relationship all round. But no. Even if they had adopted a proper rapport between doctor and nurse I still would have to say that that would not have prevented the murders. Mone had spent time in Smith's ward and he managed to con Smith with his smile and willingness to do anything asked.

They conned everyone.

Following the public inquiry Dr Loweg's internal inquiry into the staff buying clothes on our black market began. Doctor Loweg seemed to have a source of information and many of us involved believed that it had come from a former patient who had been released at his recommendation. Dr Loweg appeared in the wards and got all the patient storemen together and told them that he wanted information from them about the buying and selling of hospital clothes. Out of the ten I was the only one who refused.

While certainly I had been involved in the black market and I would have been glad to get out, how could I trust Dr Loweg? He hadn't made any guarantees. I had already served over thirty-five years in various mental institutions and I knew the score. If I had given evidence and then not got out what would my life have been then? I couldn't have taken the years of victimization which would have inevitably followed. There are those who would argue that I had become institutionalized. That wasn't the case at all. The only life I had really known was in institutions but that doesn't mean you have to become institutionalized. I was able to adapt my life to the system and in many cases adapt the system to suit my life, so while I couldn't say that I was happy in Carstairs, I had my own way of life. As it turned out, the other nine were eventually released and I served a further eleven years in Carstairs.

Looking back I have been asked whether, with hindsight, I would have been better to take the chance. After all, in the outside world eleven years is a long time. Not in the system. Owing to the fact that you are not told how long you will be in a mental institution, that you're just there until you're 'better', the brain very quickly avoids thinking about time. Unlike a prison sentence when you know you are sentenced to five years and each day brings you closer to release, in mental hospitals, as you don't know your release date, you would really drive yourself mad if you kept thinking about what date you would be let out. Even simple things are planned well in advance. It can take up to three months to get what you want by planning, planting the seeds of thought in a nurse's or doctor's mind and then achieving the end result. Three months in the system is merely a moment in time.

Of course I wanted out. I wanted to show that I could survive in the outside world and that the last time was just a mistake which wouldn't happen again. But I was fearful, if I was let out so soon after returning, that should I make the same mistake again, then that coupled with the fact that I had grassed on the nurses would have meant that life would have been hell.

I should like to add, though, that in my own way I had a loyalty, perhaps misguided, towards the staff and as I felt that the inquiry was at a stupid time and was only to get back at the staff for their treatment of the doctors following their being locked out after the Incident, then I wasn't prepared to take part in it.

When the detectives began interviewing there certainly was a buzz about the Hospital. The staff really were on tenterhooks, coupled with anger that they were being investigated at all. One of them told me that they felt that the job they did, for which they didn't consider they were well enough paid, meant that if there were any perks then so be it. I told him that he was absolutely right. I believe we had the conversation while he was buying some clothes from me!

I was the last to be interviewed. I was taken down to an office in the administration block and it was the first time I experienced the 'good and the bad' routine. There were two detectives and the younger one said to me, 'OK, Laing, we're here about the thefts of hospital property and patients selling goods to the staff.' There were no pleasantries at all.

'Gentlemen,' I said, 'you've come to the wrong person. If I saw staff stealing I would immediately report it.'

He got quite annoyed at me. 'You smoke a lot, don't you?' he growled.

'Oh yes,' I replied.

'Then how do you get the money for tobacco?'

'Well, sir, I go around collecting the empty lemonade bottles and take them to the shop in the grounds and get the money for tobacco.'

All the time during the questioning the older one would interject with phrases like, 'Come on, Jimmy, we're only trying to help you help yourself. You know if you help us the doctors have said that you might be released early.'

Then the younger one said, 'You get on well with the staff, don't you?' and then at that moment threw in a wobbler. I didn't know that a member of staff had told them that he had got a pair of boots from me. 'What about the boots you gave to a member of staff? Did he give you a couple of fags for them?'

I replied, 'Gentlemen, you're on the wrong track there. I never sold anything to the staff.'

'Well, what about the suits you have here? Nice ones, are they?' asked the younger one. And at that stage the older one brought in a black dinner suit.

I remember exactly the circumstances surrounding that incident. A nurse had asked another storeman for a new black suit and he had come to me to swap some clothes to make up the suit. I had had the right size of jacket but not the right size of trousers so we did a swap. In the end he got four ounces of tobacco for it and he shared it with me. But I wasn't prepared to say anything at that time to the detectives.

Then the older one said, 'Would you like a lager?'

I thought, 'Here we go, the softening-up procedure.' I said, 'Oh, come, come, gentlemen, in a hospital like this with me on tranquillizers, certainly not.'

'Well, where did you get the six cans you offered to another patient in exchange for some clothes?' asked the younger one.

I remembered this had happened in Erin ward some years previously and I remembered which patient had been involved. He must have been the one who grassed on us all. I again told them I didn't know what he was talking about.

'So you are a good patient, honest and above board?' he said.

'You've got it in one,' I replied.

At the end of the interview he wrote out a piece of paper and flung it across the desk to me. The words on it were 'I, James Laing, hereby swear that I have not seen or taken part in the stealing of hospital property. Nor have I taken alcohol or tobacco in exchange for hospital property.'

'There, does that make you happy then?' asked the younger one.

I replied that happy wasn't the correct word. I had told only the truth. I then asked if the interview was over and said that I wanted to say something. Their eyes lit up. I think they thought that I was going to spill the beans. I told them that I thought that the whole inquiry was completely valueless and at an inopportune time considering what had happened recently at the Hospital. At the end of the day it would have cost a lot of time, money and anguish and the end result would be zero. His reply was, 'Get out.'

I was right, though; no-one was charged and while the staff were obviously relieved there was a great deal of animosity which was to continue for many years to come.

12

Boxed In

In 1979 Scottish Television arrived at Carstairs State Hospital to make a documentary. For some weeks previous to their arrival I had heard rumours that they might be coming. The staff members had been talking about it and saying that they were apprehensive about letting cameras into Carstairs. It had been three years since the Incident and although things were calm there was still no ground parole so there was still a great element of concentration on security. The staff union, the SPOA, was still against ground parole and there wasn't a great deal of co-operation between them and the management. I heard that it had taken many weeks of preparation and discussion between Scottish Television and the authorities before permission was given to allow them to film. I also heard that the Chairman of the Board, George Robertson, and Professor McCrae were the ones who were all for it but there were some against it. Some of the nurses felt that it would stir things up and that it wouldn't be good for the patients. I thought it more likely that if there was any stirring up it would have been good for the patients and maybe not so good for the nurses and that's what they were worried about.

One day before the filming began Dr Loweg came into my ward and told me that I had been selected to speak to the television people. 'I think that you are the best person to speak on the patients' behalf,' he said. At that time it has to be said that things were improving and I decided that it was the best thing to promote the Hospital. I knew that I wouldn't be allowed to say anything derogatory about the staff or conditions as Dr Loweg had told me that the film would be checked by Scottish Office officials before it went out and that they would cut out anything they didn't like.

Before the filming began we were all told to be on our best behaviour and that anyone who tried to talk to the television crew without permission would be dealt with severely. Of course we weren't told 'officially' but a word here and there was all that was needed. There was great excitement in the Hospital the day the television crew arrived. We were able to watch them filming in the grounds and heard about them filming in the occupational therapy workshops and various other areas. Eventually they arrived at my ward and I made tea for them and showed them my collection of autographed photographs which I had acquired over the years. It had been a hobby of mine writing off to the stars and getting their photographs. One good thing had been the authorities' decision that we need not use the name Carstairs State Hospital in our address.

It would have certainly been offputting to reply to someone in a mental hospital. My address was Villa Clyde, Carnwath, Lanarkshire.

Once we had had some tea I was allowed to show the crew around the ward, always with the charge nurse beside me. Then we came to the interview. I wasn't allowed to be seen in vision, that was one of the rules which the Scottish Office had laid down when permission to film was given. I said in the interview that things were progressing very well since the Incident. Then there was a question about violence in the Hospital. I knew that I would have to side-step this question. I could hardly say, with the charge nurse standing outside listening to all that was going on, that a small minority of the staff were adroit with their hands. I said that if someone was coming towards you seemingly about to hit you then you would try to defend yourself. But that was taken as a criticism of the Hospital and in the final version of the programme that bit was cut out.

While I had decided that the best thing was to promote the Hospital, for all concerned, I saw it as a way to promote myself. It was a kind of gateway for me. It proved that I could be trusted to do as I was asked by the authorities. But it shouldn't be thought that I just wanted glory for myself, I wanted things to improve at the Hospital. Ground parole was essential for the patients. It would give them something to work towards; something which would improve their lives. I had to add, though, that it was a privilege that had to be worked for, not to be received as of right.

When the programme came out on television I received congratulatory calls from all over the Hospital. Even the staff thought I had done a good job. It was obvious from their comments that I had said the right things. Whether or not that would be classed as a 'good job' was debatable.

A few days after the programme Dr Loweg came into the ward and told me that I had been very good. I remember Dr Loweg's contribution. It showed that underneath he did understand psychiatric patients. Why couldn't he show that side to us? He had said, 'To be bad is bad, to be mad is bad, but to be bad and mad is the curse of the gods.' How true. He also spoke about the possibility of curing the psychiatric patient. His theory was that the person who committed even the most heinous crime was really a different person 'inside' from the 'outer' person. It was his job to find the 'normal' person inside the mind of the psychiatric patient. So he had the theory right; the main trouble was that he was unable to practise what he preached in a more understanding way.

After the first film the staff asked Scottish Television back to make another programme about their concerns for the future. They certainly said some positive things but it was interesting that the younger ones were those who were more interested in changing the regime. The older ones kept harping on about their fears about ground parole and bringing up the case of the little son of the then Superintendent who had been murdered by a patient back in the 1950s. My God, couldn't they ever forget! Imagine bringing that back up nearly thirty years later. No wonder things didn't move forward very quickly at Carstairs. All in all the patients, and some of the staff, thought that the staff interviewed put on a pretty poor show. As they were all members of the SPOA it wouldn't have done for them all to say that everything in the garden was rosy, but they could have said that things weren't as bad as they were sometimes portrayed. They put over the attitude that everything may be fine today, but what of tomorrow? They would quote hypothetical examples, such as if we had ground parole and there were some patients walking in the grounds at the same time as the secretaries were crossing over to the administration block then they might attack them. They never mentioned that we might just say hallo to them. It is certainly true that there are those who could never be trusted; the silent, devious types, like Mone and McCulloch. But if the staff at places like the State Hospital are of the right calibre then they should be able to spot the ones who are suitable for, say, ground parole and those who are not. An example of being able to tell the difference would come from a simple incident such as one that happened to me. One day I was playing snooker and a nurse came up behind me. He had been niggling me all day and pushed the cue as I was about to play. He thought it was a great laugh. My reaction would be to blow up. The types to watch were the ones who would just take it all with a mutter.

13

Closer to Freedom

For the next four years from when the television
crew were at Carstairs life improved gradually. We
started receiving different types of patients: not just
the long-term patients but those who were being
sent there for a fright. We had one particular patient
from Dundee who came in as a very violent person,
but as treatment procedures were improving within
six months he was out. Nowadays a person can
be sent to Carstairs for as little as three months
and then out. It was also used as a frightener for
people who were on drugs. There was one young
lad who was never violent but was committing
crimes while on heroin. Three months in Carstairs
certainly sorted him out. He never returned. Unlike
the old days when there were no individuals, just
patients, in the early Eighties the authorities began
to realize that everyone had a talent and developing
that talent would eventually lead to the individual
being cured. I can say without reservation that when
I recall the days of Baldovan, Murthly, Gartloch,

the CLD and the early days at Carstairs they bear no comparison to the regime today. I'm not saying that it became a paradise on earth. There were still the rotten minority of staff but it was good to see how things were getting better.

But you still had to play the system at its own game. While the authorities were prepared to accept a bit of intelligence the last thing they wanted was some 'smart arse' telling them what to do. So you kept your eyes open, mouth closed and bided your time. I wasn't alone in all of this. There were others who were as strong-willed. We would not think of ourselves as better than the nurses and certainly we never thought that they were better than us but we had to let them think that they were better than us. We patients were mere mortals compared to the nurses. Inside we were in turmoil feeling that we were equals yet outside giving the impression that we were subservient to them.

In about 1984 I withdrew from my storekeeping and moved to a job in the administration ward. I still handled clothing and, one could say, kept my hand in by selling the odd item to a nurse when they required it.

There were some poor souls in that administration ward. It was the first ward they were brought to when they arrived at Carstairs. It took me back to my early days and I tried to make their lives as bearable as possible. The nurses could be very harsh with them. I used to try to tell them that they had fathers and sons just like these patients and that these people were at their lowest ebb. How did they know that something wasn't going to happen to one of their sons or fathers the next day? Some would listen, others paid no attention.

By this time Dr Loweg had left Carstairs. I well remember our last meeting. He came into the ward. 'How are you today, young man?' he asked. 'You know I'm leaving today but I just thought I'd tell you something before I left. You know you shouldn't be sitting here talking to me today. You should be out. If you had told the truth about the staff at the inquiry into the theft of hospital property then you would have been out today. But you decided to stick with the staff and you're still here.'

I tried to tell him why I had done it, that I hadn't long been back in as well as the fact that I really didn't trust him or anyone else.

'But you've been here a further ten years, James,' he said.

'When you've been in institutions as long as I have, Dr Loweg, then ten years is not long,' I replied. I also tried to explain to him what it would have been like to have spent a year or more before getting out under a regime which knew that I had grassed on one of the nurses.

I then told him that another reason I had my job in the store and in the kitchen was that, in many ways, I was in charge of my own life. I wasn't prepared to give that up without a guarantee of release. For all the years he had dealt with me he had learned little about the real me. He didn't realize that for someone who had spent at that time forty-six years in institutions the pleasures in life were getting up in the morning, making my own tea, being of the highest privilege, being able to move about the ward and in and out of my storeroom. These were the trappings of high order for me. I wasn't prepared to give all that up.

He looked at me in amazement. Even though he was dealing with patients on a daily basis he would return home each evening. Until you have actually been inside places like Carstairs as a patient it is impossible to understand what goes on in the mind of a patient. He obviously, despite his vast experience, had never really *learned*. To people on the outside the thought of spending ten years in an institution when you didn't have to would seem horrific but, as I have said before, time means nothing at Carstairs. If it takes another ten years to get out then that's what it takes.

I knew that he would retire eventually and that when a new psychiatrist came along he or she would evaluate my case from the first time we met. Many of the modern psychiatrists will read up the case notes for the past then put them to one side and make their own judgement. This is a very fortunate progression. Before Dr Loweg left I had told him during our last conversation that I would be out in two or three years.

My new psychiatrist was Dr Ann McDonald, who was in her mid-thirties. In the initial few weeks we didn't say much to each other, merely pleasantries. Then one morning one of the nurses came out of the regular meetings she had with the staff and told me that they had been discussing my case. 'She wants you out,' he said. The next day two other nurses, who were nurses in the real sense of the word, Ronnie Leith and Ronnie McVicar, came to me to tell me that they thought that things were going well for me and to stay calm.

Then towards the end of 1984 I was told that the majority of the nurses at the regular evaluation meetings wanted me completely released but that Dr McDonald wanted me to go out via an open mental hospital. I felt really good that at long last I was heading for freedom but I had to now be very careful about my conduct. One mistake could set me back years. The months that followed were the biggest strain I had ever experienced.

I was taken to see Dr Radcliffe and the Superintendent and at this meeting everything was wonderful. We even had coffee brought in on a tray for us. He told me that they were thinking of sending me to Crighton Royal Hospital or to Murray Royal Hospital. I told him that I would prefer to go to Murray Royal but he said that they had to have an option just in case Murray Royal couldn't take me. He finished the interview by saying, 'I won't see you again and I wish you well.'

I was still working in the administration ward and I put myself completely into my work. In my own mind I was atoning for some of the sins of the past. Not that I had ever been a bad patient but now I tried as hard as I could to help the new patients who were arriving. There were some poor souls there and, as I had in previous institutions, I made sure that they were bathed and shaved and gave them what little self-respect I could. I was almost working as an auxiliary nurse and I enjoyed it.

Then, unexpectedly, I almost blotted my copybook. It was a trivial thing. I realized I was being wound up and made sure that I didn't take the bait. I was working in the kitchens one day and as usual I was being very particular about the cleanliness of everything. I set out the table for the staff. By this time the staff were using the same utensils as the patients. One of the patients who was helping out in the kitchen came in to tell me that one of the nurses, Willie from Lanark, was complaining that his spoon was dirty. Now I knew that that wasn't true, I always checked the utensils before laying the table. In the old days I would have had an argument about it but I decided that I would take it through the 'correct channels'. It should be added that the staff weren't supposed to be fed with hospital food – after all it was for the patients – but they made sure that they got their share. How the authorities weren't able to work out what quantity of food was required exactly is beyond me. It wouldn't be that difficult. I suppose it had been going on so long it was just accepted practice.

I stood for a moment, and then walked out of the kitchen down the corridor to the little staff room. I walked straight up to Willie and asked him what the hell was going on. One of the other nurses began to laugh and said, 'I told you it would get him going.' I turned to them and said, 'This is the last time you'll do that to me or anyone else as far as I'm concerned. It was OK in the old days but not now. One more example of this and I'll go to the chief staff nurse and then to the police.' Their faces changed at that and I walked out. I must admit that I was a bit shaken up at that but I felt it had to be done. I hadn't lost my temper. I wasn't violent in any way and I didn't even raise my voice.

Later that day I was about to go into the staff office to clean up and I heard Willie complaining about the incident to Jock Reid, one of the charge nurses. He told him that it should be put on my Kardex file that I had spoken in a bad way to a nurse. 'Come off it, Willie,' said Jock, 'it's Jimmy Laing you're dealing with here. Do you think that anyone is going to believe you that Jimmy became outspoken for no apparent reason when he's only got a few months left to do? Dinnae be so daft.' After Willie had left I went into the office and casually asked Jock if I was going to be reported for the incident. Jock smiled and said, 'What do you think, Jimmy?' Then he added, 'By the way, well done.' Now he wasn't congratulating me for having taken down a member of staff, although there was a bit of that, he was congratulating me on keeping control of myself and being able to assert myself at the same time.

About a month later I learned that I was being transferred to Murray Royal Hospital in Perth. It came about one day when Dr McDonald came round to my ward. She came into the kitchen and I gave her a cup of tea. I was on tenterhooks. Was she going to tell me? I daren't ask in case I was seen as being forward. Or was she going to keep me waiting yet another day? She turned to me and almost as an aside she said, 'You're going to Murray Royal on the twenty-seventh of August.'

I just wanted to let rip a blood-curdling scream of ecstasy. At long last I was going to be released. It is hard to imagine the delight that was racing through my body. Almost fifteen years had passed since I had been sent back to Carstairs from Inverness – for a 'short time' and at long last I was getting out. Yes, I wanted to scream and shout but I couldn't let myself do that. This was a testing time for me and if I went over the top they might just change their minds and keep me in. I said to Dr McDonald, 'Oh, that's great news, I'm so glad it's all worked out for me. Thank you very much, Doctor, for all your help.' She smiled and said it was her pleasure and she hoped that I'd do well.

I have suffered a lot in the years I was inside but nothing like the suffering that I went through in those last four months before my release. I prayed that I would get through each day without incident. For the first time, time was preying on my mind. Now that I knew my release date each day seemed an eternity. Thank God it was only for four months. That was bad enough. Some nights my mind would play tricks on me, my imagination would run riot. I'd convince myself that everything was all right and then I would hear one of the nurses patrolling the corridor. Would he come into my room? Had I done something that day that they were going to complain about? Would he come up to my door and give it a kick, just for the hell of it, as they had done in the past? If I got up in the morning and complained would that go against me? All these things bounced around inside my head until I fell asleep. In the morning I'd awaken to the new day and begin to plan what I would do to ensure that that day would go smoothly and that there would be no slip-ups.

About two weeks before my release date an incident occurred that I have lived with since and which has tormented me ever since it happened. We had a particular patient in the admission ward who was in Carstairs as one of the many patients who was dumped there. He had a habit of keeping some of his bread from his meals and throwing it out of the window in his room for the birds. This was frowned upon. One day he was caught throwing the bread out by an enrolled nurse who called in another nurse, saying, 'Come and see this. What a bloody mess you've made outside.' Then I heard them slapping the patient and eventually beating him up. The next day, Thursday, was bathing day, and one of the nurses announced that we would get as many bathed as possible in the morning as there was a good film on television that afternoon. I hadn't said anything to anybody about the beating but Jock Reid came on duty and he saw that the patient was black and blue with bruises. Jock immediately called his superior officer, George Tait, who was the group charge nurse. George arrived and said that he was having nothing to do with it and called in the principal nursing officer Ian MacKenzie. He in turn called in Dr McDonald who called in the local GP from Carnwath who gave the patient a full examination. He pronounced that there was evidence the patient had been badly beaten. Dr McDonald called in the police. What a difference to the old days. In times past the whole incident would have been hushed up, but not in modern times, thank God. When the police arrived the patient told them that he had been beaten up for throwing bread out of the window to the birds. 'I feed them every day,' he said. He was a poor soul. However, an inquiry was immediately started and the union agreed that it would co-operate.

The police organized an identity parade of eight nurses from around the hospital and the patient was asked to pick out the nurse involved. He went up and down the line and picked out the one who had beaten him up. The other one wasn't there and as he hadn't actually taken part in the beating he was allowed to go free. The nurse involved was immediately suspended from duty. The police then began to question the other patients in the ward about the beating. Eventually they came to me. 'Good afternoon, Mr Laing,' said the policeman. 'We are making inquiries into the alleged beating that took place and we want to know if you have any knowledge of it. Did you hear any noises, screams or shouts?' My life flashed in front of me. I had just come from the bedside of a very young patient called Sammy. He had been sent to Carstairs as he was unmanageable at the other hospital he had been in. I had spent a lot of time with him as his story was so close to my own. I thought of him and the future that lay ahead. I thought of my own future and the fact that I was getting out in two weeks' time.

Later my reply was to tear holes inside me. 'I don't know anything about any beatings, sir,' I replied. 'I didn't hear anything at all. We have a patient here who tends to shout a lot, perhaps that's what I heard.' I actually wanted to believe that. My God, what a coward. All those years fighting for my own rights and those in the system and at the end I let myself and the others down. Why did I do it? Yes, I did it for myself but I also did it for Sammy. If I had told the truth all hell would have broken loose. The system, by this time, was changing, it had changed a lot, and was still progressing. I was leaving. Was I going to leave that young boy behind to the life I had suffered? No, I had to leave him to survive in a system which, I hoped, would provide him with a better life than I had ever had inside. But I was sick within myself. I excused myself and went to my room where I wept my heart out. In spite of my good intentions to help Sammy, I had betrayed my fellow patients. Self-preservation had eventually taken me to this awful stage. If I had spoken out I could have been kept at Carstairs for months afterwards for internal inquiries.

Eventually the inquiry gave its result. No action was taken against the nurse in question as the case against him could not be proved. A whitewash. There was no court case as it was felt that Carstairs was doing so well that something like that would have set back the progress which was being made. It has to be said that the incidents of violence in those days, 1985, were few and far between even in Medwin ward and I heard later that the SPOA had met with the Board to discuss the problem and it had been intimated that the spirit of co-operation wouldn't be maintained if the incident had been taken to court. One may ask how an incident such as that could be covered up? The Hospital is covered by the Official Secrets Act and once the authorities have decided that no action will be taken that is the end of the matter. While I believe that the Official Secrets Act can, and should, apply to patients' cases I do not believe that it should be used to protect someone who should not be allowed back to work at the State Hospital after he has assaulted a patient. Some things never change at Carstairs.

The nurse in question came back to the ward the day after the inquiry delivered its result and I half suspected that he would have his tail between his legs. Nothing could be further from the truth. I was in my room when he arrived and he came to the door and shouted, 'Right, you bastard, your fucking holiday's over. Get out of there.'

I said to myself, 'I'm having none of this.' I followed him down to the staff office and said to him, 'You're working here today because I lied for you. I heard you beating up that patient yet I told the police that I had heard nothing.' His face turned chalk-white. 'If you carry on with this kind of treatment then I'll be forced to go to the authorities and tell them all I know.'

'OK, Jimmy, I understand, it won't happen again,' he said.

However, one of the charge nurses, Frank Scott, came up to me and we had a long chat about it and later he also spoke to the nurse in question and that was the end of the problem.

By now I had only three days to go and Frank had suggested that I took some time off from working in the admission ward to get myself ready for going out. My initial reaction was to refuse. I was still officially based in Forth ward and that is for long-term patients. I knew that when someone is leaving it affects the patients to varying degrees. Some are elated that a patient is getting out and some can crack up. Eventually I decided to go back to Forth with only forty-eight hours to go. I went back to my room, packed up my clothes and remained there for the next twenty-four hours apart from going out to the toilet. I didn't want to see anybody; not so much the patients, rather I didn't want to see or speak to the nurses. I didn't want to listen to the inanities of their conversation or overhear them saying, 'Oh, he'll be back.' I'd heard it all before and didn't want to listen to it ever again.

I read all day and I had my food brought up to me by another patient. On the final night, the twenty-sixth, surprisingly I was able to sleep. I laid my head down about midnight and slept straight through until seven the next morning. That morning, 27 August 1985, the nurse came up to open the doors and I got up, washed and shaved and dressed upstairs in my room, and waited for the car to arrive to take me out. Eventually the phone call came that the car was on its way and I went downstairs. I just wanted to get away. I didn't want any ceremony from anyone, just a quick goodbye to those I knew best — the patients.

As we got towards the gates I began to panic slightly. Were the papers in order? One mistake and they would refuse to let me pass. But the gates slid open and we passed through. I was finally out of Carstairs. What a relief it was. I knew that I still had to do time at Murray Royal but that was a 'real' mental hospital. Not like Carstairs which is a hospital in name only. Before getting out I had been on 'training for freedom' days – out with a nurse to Edinburgh – to see how I got on. Those had been fine but you always knew you had to come back to Carstairs. Now I was really heading for freedom. I suppose that it would be expected that I wanted to get out of the car, breathe in the fresh air and maybe even go for a walk in the fields, but that was not the case. I was delighted to be out but, while I don't want to be considered exceptional, I had kept up to date with what was going on in the world. I knew what the outside was all about. My room had overlooked the long Lanark Road, there was less than a field between it and the Hospital and, strange though it may seem, I had been able to mentally take down the fence that lay between it and the road. I always knew I would get out and that fence was not going to stand in my way.

All my problems at Carstairs were now behind me. I was leaving and I was determined never to return. I didn't even look back at the place as I left.

14

Eleanor

The journey from Carstairs to Murray Royal took about an hour. On the way there Ian Horne, the nurse delegated to accompany me, and I chatted about 'normal' things. Not one word was mentioned about the State Hospital. My time in Carstairs was ashes now as far as I was concerned. My thoughts were all for Murray Royal and how I would fit in there and ensure that I would gain my full release as soon as possible.

I was fortunate that I had already met the charge nurse and the sister who would be dealing with me and my doctor, Dr Kirk. They had come down to Carstairs when it was decided that they could fit me into their hospital. We had chatted and sized each other up, in the friendliest way. They had explained all about their hospital, the regime and all that went with it. They certainly had impressed me with their care and attention to detail and they were a delight to meet.

We arrived at Murray Royal and I was shown into the admission office. Dr Kirk passed through and merely said hallo. All psychiatrists like you to 'stew' for a while. I think they must be taught that as their first lesson at University. 'Let them wait for a while before you talk to them.' It was about a week before I had my first interview with her.

The staff had been told who I was and where I came from but the patients hadn't. Eventually I let those know who asked. The staff obviously had been well briefed about my case. They were all very pleasant. I was put into a mixed ward. During the day we all sat together and ate together in the dining room. Sleeping arrangements were, of course, separate. I had been asked at Carstairs how I thought I would cope with a mixed ward, having spent so many years without the company of women. I told them that I had no fears about it. They seemed to be worried but again this is a throwback to the old days of psychiatry where everything to do with mental illness is in some way connected with sex. Maybe they thought I would go off the deep end at the sight of a woman!

I fitted in well with everyone. I found out later that there was another patient from Carstairs, a chap from Aberdeen who had committed a capital offence and they had trouble with him when he was mixing with the women. He had been on the verge of being sent back to Carstairs quite a few times but fortunately the hospital had managed to pull him back into line. These days mental hospitals which take patients from Carstairs don't like having to send patients back to Carstairs. It's admitting defeat and that's a testimony to the changes in mental health care today. In the past they would have immediately sent someone back if they had caused any trouble and the patient would never have progressed.

The life at Murray Royal was extremely pleasant compared to that at Carstairs. I spent those summer days reading and going for walks in the grounds. Some days a nurse and I would walk up Kinnoull Hill. For the first time I felt I really was being made ready for the outside world.

The following March I decided to leave Murray Royal. I felt that I was ready to make my way in the world and so I walked out of the hospital and went to Edinburgh. I had no fears of retribution if I was caught as things had changed a great deal since the days of Gartloch when my absconding had eventually led to my being sent to the CLD. I knew within myself that the authorities wouldn't send me back to Carstairs.

I quickly found lodgings in Edinburgh, having seen an advert in a shop window near to Merchiston School. The house was owned by a Pakistani and the room was quite comfortable. I had some money on me and I gave him a five-pound note as a deposit. I decided that I would do everything above board and I decided to register with the local doctor. His surgery was a large bungalow nearby and I made an appointment to see him. At the appointment I told him that I was from Murray Royal and he asked me who my doctor was. 'Dr Kirk,' I replied. 'Oh, you're one of Dr Kirk's patients. Very good then,' said the doctor. He didn't even ask me if and when I had been released, which at the time I found a bit surprising, but I wasn't going to say anything that would spoil my plan. From there I went to the Social Security offices to register for employment. While I had some money saved up over the years my bank book was still at Murray Royal. They wouldn't let you keep that and gave it to you only when you wanted money out of the account and then you had to return it. I told the counter clerk at the DHSS office that I needed money to tide me over and she asked how much I had been earning. I explained that I had been earning just over four pounds a week at Murray Royal in the occupational therapy unit. She said that they could give me only thirty-two pounds that week and to return in the afternoon for the Giro cheque. I walked around the centre of Edinburgh for the next few hours making my plans and working out where I would get employment. I knew that my stint in the garages would stand me in good stead and I made a note to contact the Stadium service station where I had worked previously to see if I could get a job there.

I returned to the DHSS office that afternoon and took my place in the queue. One of the chaps in front of me moved up to the window and the clerkess came out with a large bundle of files. I noticed that the chap was deaf and that the clerkess was finding it hard going to understand him and make herself understood. As I had taught myself the rudiments of the deaf and dumb language at Carstairs, when we had an old deaf patient in our ward, I offered to help out. I asked her what she wanted to know and translated her questions and his answers. After he left I resumed my place at the end of the queue. Eventually I was the only person left in the waiting room and the clerkess got up to go. I went forward to the window and called her to ask her what had happened to my Giro cheque. 'What's your name?' she asked. 'James McLaughlin Laing,' I replied and at that moment I felt a hand on my shoulder. Standing behind me was a policeman. 'C'mon, Jimmy, they're looking for you back at Murray Royal.' My heart sank. Caught again. No wonder the doctor didn't make much of the fact that I was from Murray Royal. He was probably on the telephone to them as soon as I left.

As soon as I returned I was taken to see Dr Kirk. While she wasn't very pleased that I had absconded she said she wouldn't hold it against me as I had gone about everything outside in the right way. I hadn't got into trouble or gone on the rampage. The fact that I had gone about things in the correct way seemed to be to my advantage. Despite these plus points I still had to remain in Murray Royal. It's part of the system that you have to do a certain amount of time in a place like Murray Royal when you've been transferred from Carstairs. It wouldn't do to let you out too quickly. Heaven forbid.

It was about this time, April 1986, that Eleanor appeared in my life. Eleanor's husband had died a year earlier and she had taken it very hard and had had a slight nervous breakdown. This necessitated her going into Murray Royal for a couple of months but she had been one of the patients who was allowed complete freedom of movement and access and was allowed into the city any time she pleased. It was the type of treatment quite frequently practised today where the hospital is used as a place of comfort and safety from the stress a patient is suffering.

She had already completed her two months and was now attending the occupational therapy department three days a week when we first met.

I learned through another patient that Eleanor liked me and wanted to meet me. We began to chat each time she was at the hospital and I began to look forward with great anticipation to her visits. But the psychiatrists did not. They immediately informed me that Eleanor was on the rebound and that our relationship wouldn't last. They were happy for us to be friends but that was to be the extent of our relationship. How patronizing! They also pointed out to me that I had never had a heterosexual relationship and that could cause all sorts of problems. My God, why couldn't they have spoken about how it would be nice to go shopping with someone, live in a house together, be companions. No. As far as the psychiatrists were concerned these things were unimportant. The only theme they were interested in was sex.

To say I wasn't concerned about that aspect of our relationship would be a lie. There was I, fifty-seven years old, and I had never had sexual intercourse with a woman. But any fears that I had were overcome by the joy of my relationship with Eleanor. For the first time in my life someone cared for me without my having to curry favour.

Throughout my life, even as a child, I had never had anyone who loved me for myself. My mother, while she had been good to me, had not been the loving type of person. She rarely, if ever, hugged or kissed me and my father certainly never showed me affection. Here now was someone who was prepared to take me at face value. During her visits we spoke about the future and I asked Eleanor to take her time. I told her all about myself, every detail, before the doctors told her about me.

Our relationship progressed all through that summer and at Christmas we got engaged. One of the nurses at Murray Royal was my niece's sister-in-law's daughter and I asked her to buy me an engagement ring with the money I had saved up. We got engaged in the canteen at Murray Royal and Eleanor's friend Rose and a friend of hers were there to celebrate with us. No champagne, just tea and biscuits!

I let it be known around the hospital and a couple of days later Dr Kirk sent for me. 'Congratulations,' she said. As I knew what was coming up I told her, before she could get it in, 'There's no question of Eleanor being on the rebound. We have spoken together and she knows all about me. She even knows that I have never had sex with a woman. She knows about my homosexuality, how it happened and why it happened. I was sure of our relationship but I was determined that she should be sure of it before we went any further.' I told Dr Kirk that Eleanor had been to her son and daughter-in-law and other members of her family. She had told them all about me and their only question to her was, 'Do you love him?' Her answer was 'Yes'.

However Dr Kirk was very cynical. The word came from St Andrew's House that we should wait for two years to see if it would work out. How on earth could it work out if I was to spend a further two years in Murray Royal? Imagine the strain that would put on both of us. And who knows what that strain could have done? It could have set me back so far that I may have cracked up. Then the authorities would have said, 'There you are. We were right all along. He couldn't cope with the relationship.' I decided that this was one thing that was not going to be stopped by the system. For over forty years the system had controlled my life: when I woke, when I ate, when I slept and even, in the early days at Carstairs, when I could go to the toilet. The system wasn't going to spoil my relationship with Eleanor. I wasn't going to lose the best thing that had ever happened to me.

In March 1987 after a great deal of planning I absconded from Murray Royal and made for Glasgow. I hadn't told Eleanor that I was going as I knew it would worry her. I checked into the Commercial Hotel and telephoned her. She was upset that I had absconded and said that she was frightened that if they caught me they might not let her come to see me. I assured her that everything would be all right and I asked her if she still wanted to marry me. 'Oh yes,' she replied.

I told her to get a copy of my birth certificate and one of her own and that I would make a date at the registry office in Glasgow. The banns were put up and the date was set. Eleanor and Rose came to Glasgow and we had arranged for one of the clerks at the registry office to act as best man. The day arrived and we were sitting in the registry office all done up in our best bib and tucker waiting to be called. About twenty minutes passed after the time set and I went up to the commissionaire and said to him that we were supposed to be married twenty minutes ago. His reply almost gave me heart failure: 'The registrar is talking to someone at St Andrew's House.'

I must have died a dozen times as I paced up and down. I thought, 'Surely this is not how it's going to end? Not at this stage, at the last hurdle.' In normal circumstances one would have kicked up a fuss and demanded to know what was going on but with my past life and the fact that I was 'on the run' from Murray Royal I couldn't say anything at all. All I could do was just pray that everything would work out fine.

Fifteen minutes later I asked again and was told that he was still on to St Andrew's House. In my mind I could see two policemen arriving to pick me up and take me back to Edinburgh, and in front of Eleanor. How would she cope with it? About ten minutes later the registrar appeared in the waiting room full of apologies. 'I'm sorry about the delay. I was on the phone to St Andrew's House,' he said. I waited with trepidation for his next words. Was he about to tell me that the wedding couldn't go ahead? He turned to us and said, 'Will the bride and groom please come into my office?' The phone call had had nothing to do with me. Everything was now OK. We went into the office and sat down and he began talking about marriage. 'We get many couples in here who have not given enough thought to marriage. If you're not sure about it then it would be better that you both get up and leave,' he said. We both told him that we had given the matter a great deal of thought and wanted to be married. He went out and called in Rose and the best man and he performed the marriage ceremony. Oh, how happy I was. All those years of incarceration in those various institutions seemed to disappear in a flash.

We went from the registry office to a nearby restaurant and had a meal as our wedding reception. It was the best day of my life.

15

Home to Perth

That night Eleanor and I checked into the Commercial Hotel as man and wife. Sex was the last thing on our minds. I think that we were both so exhausted after the traumas of the wedding that we just fell asleep. For my part I felt that I wanted to wait until we were together in our own home, setting up for a life together. I wanted it to be special.

Eleanor returned home the next day after I had told her of my plans. I was going to go back to the Murray Royal. I knew that if I walked into the hospital it would be a plus point in my favour. On the Saturday I went across to Edinburgh to Eleanor's home and spent the day with her. She kissed me as I left and I walked up to Murray Royal. When I walked into the ward the duty nurse's reaction was merely, 'Oh, hallo. You're back with us are you, Jimmy? I'd better let them know you're here.' No reprimand, nothing.

Dr Kirk was informed that I was back but she ignored me. I don't know why she did this. It was a very trying period for me but I was determined not to show it. Eleanor came up to see me every night from five till eight, and those visits made all the difference. But she went through the mill. She got it into her mind that if they kept me in the hospital they might try to annul the marriage on the grounds that I was insane. I kept reassuring her that everything was OK but she had a hard time of it.

About six weeks after I returned I was told to attend one of Dr Kirk's group meetings. 'Oh, I see we have a stranger with us this morning. Good morning, James,' she said, as she walked in. I kept calm and kept my mouth shut. At the end of the meeting she told me to wait behind as she wanted to talk to me. I thought, 'Here it comes.'

'What in the hell are you playing at?' she asked.

'It's no longer a game, Doctor,' I replied, 'I'm a married man, I have responsibilities now.'

'Do you want to say anything to me?' she asked.

I said, 'I have been given something more precious than I have ever had and there is no way anyone, not even you will take that away from me.'

'Well, Dr Radcliffe from the Scottish Office will be coming up in a couple of weeks' time. We'll see what he has to say about it,' she said. Apart from that she made no comments about my marriage, why I had absconded or anything else. She didn't even explain why she had ignored me for the best part of six weeks.

That night Eleanor and I were sitting alone in the canteen when one of the nurses came in and closed the door. He came up to our table and told me that I had nothing to worry about. 'Everything's going to be all right,' he said. From the next day on things seemed to change. I began to be treated as a person rather than as one of the patients. I was allowed to go where I pleased in or out of the hospital as long as I returned at night.

While some would see this as still being under restrictions, to me it was freedom. Yes, I had to return at night but I was able to be with Eleanor during the day whenever I wanted to. We were able to go shopping or just walk around. About two weeks after Dr Kirk's meeting Dr Radcliffe arrived at the hospital. I had been told that he would see me and I asked if Eleanor would be allowed to come to the meeting with me. They agreed.

I was slightly nervous before the meeting, as was Eleanor, but we were confident that we would win through. Dr Radcliffe began talking about the difficulties of marriage and all the problems which went with it under normal circumstances and that how in my case it might even be more difficult. I told him that I would be able to cope with someone like Eleanor at my side.

'Well, what I'm going to do, James, is for the first month I'm going to allow you to stay away at the weekends and then after that we'll review the situation,' he said.

I was thrilled. Eleanor asked me afterwards why I hadn't asked him to let me out permanently, a natural reaction. I explained to her that you didn't question the system, you merely did as you were told. You never asked in case you were let down and I certainly didn't want to be let down at this stage. For the next four months I was able to spend every weekend at home with Eleanor. We had a great time getting to know each other.

There were some quirky little things which happened, though. I had spent so long in regimes where you had to ask for permission to do anything that this was still second nature to me. One day Eleanor and I went shopping for some clothes for me and I asked the assistant in the first shop we went into if I could have her permission to look at some ties. Her strange look reminded me that I wasn't inside any more. I didn't have to ask. Another instance was the first time that Eleanor told me to take some money out of her purse to buy some shopping; I brought the purse through to her and asked her to take the money out. Mentally I was still attuned to a life where someone could accuse you of stealing if you did not have a witness to prove that you had an official reason for taking something.

Then on 1 November 1986 I was told to telephone Eleanor and tell her that I was coming home. I walked out of that hospital forty-seven years and two months after I had first been sent to Baldovan for being an unmanageable child. Initially I had to report to a social worker on a weekly basis and see a doctor every six weeks but as time progressed the contact with them both diminished.

Eleanor and I decided that we would move back to Perth. Coincidentally both of us had been born there. We found a house and began to build a home together. It was something I had always dreamed about and although I was determined to achieve it as time went on in Carstairs there were times when I thought it would never happen.

Like every man and wife we have had our ups and downs. Life wouldn't be normal without them. But now I have a wife to stand up for me. Something I have never had before. I am treated like any normal human being. I go about my business just like everyone else. I can have my good days and bad days without it being seen as something which should be commented on and written down in a Kardex file. I am able to do what I want when I want: able to lie in my bed if I want to or to get up early; to go to bed when I decide rather than someone deciding it for me.

I have often been asked why I am not bitter after all my experiences. Bitterness is a cancer which will go right through your body and eventually take over and destroy you. I am not bitter. I am angry, though, that there was no power of redress in the old days. There was no way that you could argue your case to try to prove that you shouldn't be in the system.

Today there are various groups interested in the welfare of mental patients which keep their plight to the forefront and that is a great step forward. Mental patients need their support particularly when they're at the lowest ebb. When you're down at rock bottom, to know that someone is interested in you gives you the necessary lift to continue living. Those like me who have suffered the old regimes know how bad it can be. The progress which is being made will continue and will bring some relief to their tormented souls.

I have also been asked if I think that my case could repeat itself even today with the greater awareness, greater parental concern and a greater overall attitude to life in general. Sadly, I think that while there are a variety of safety nets around, there are those who will still fall through. God help them.

Postscript

When I was released in November 1986, I considered myself a free man. But when enquiries were made about my case for the making of a television documentary on my life, the Scottish Office in Edinburgh immediately telephoned my psychiatrist. She advised me against participating in the programme, saying it was 'for my own good'.

I might no longer have been an in-patient, but I felt then that I was still very much in the System.

However, I am pleased to inform readers of my book that I am at last a completely free person. On 12 July 1990, the Secretary of State for Scotland appended his signature to a document permitting me to become a 'normal' member of society.

Freedom has not been without its difficulties, in that, though I would like to work to support myself and my wife, I have so far found a job unobtainable. But I would like to say thank you to the very kind people who have written to me, since the publication of my book in hardcover, giving me encouragement – not forgetting all the people who have stopped me in the street to wish me well, and many others in my home town. To them I would say, in answer to their question: no, to date I have received no compensation.

However, there would appear to be a better future. At the time of writing my case for compensation is being taken up, and a television production company is working on a film about my life. And Eleanor and I are still together.

Perth 1992

About Mind

MIND is the leading mental health charity in England and Wales. It works for a better life for people diagnosed, labelled or treated as mentally ill and campaigns for their right to lead an active and valued life in the community.

In all its activities MIND stresses the particular needs of black people, women and other oppressed groups.

Drawing on the knowledge and skills both of people who provide and use the mental health services, MIND has established itself not only as the largest independent provider of good quality care in the community, but also as an influential commentator on government policy in all areas of mental health.

MIND
(National Association for Mental Health)
22 Harley Street, London W1N 2ED

THE DARK ROMANCE OF DIAN FOSSEY
by Harold Hayes

'Hayes' dramatic style and tense narrative make an already striking story vivid and compelling'
Time Out

On a December morning in 1985, residents of the Karisoke Centre for Mountain Gorilla Research in the tiny African state of Rwanda woke to learn that Dian Fossey was dead – her head split open by a machete.

Harold Hayes' remarkable book explores the life of Dian Fossey, who abandoned her career as an occupational therapist in Kentucky to live in Africa amongst the last remaining mountain gorillas. Going further than any previous account, including the popular film *Gorillas in the Mist*, Hayes captures the nature of the all-too-human woman who, without scientific training, nevertheless persuaded the eminent Louis Leakey to send her to Africa, a continent she had visited only once.

Hayes describes her strange childhood, her time in Kentucky, her years in Rwanda and the Belgian Congo, and her turbulent romantic life, including her affair with the married photographer whose departure almost destroyed her; and, unforgettably, Fossey's battle against poachers to keep the mountain gorillas alive. Above all, he shows how the turmoil inside Dian Fossey grew into self-destruction and unpredictable fury. Drawing on years of research and interviews, *The Dark Romance of Dian Fossey* draws us into the heart of Africa and the mind of an extraordinary woman.

'Bolts the reader to the page with velvet rivets'
Kirkus Reviews

0 552 13879 7

THE GOD SQUAD
by Paddy Doyle

His mother died from cancer in 1955. His father committed suicide shortly thereafter. Paddy Doyle was sentenced in an Irish district court to be detained in an industrial school for eleven years. He was four years old . . .

Paddy Doyle's prize-winning bestseller, THE GOD SQUAD, is both a moving and terrifying testament to the institutionalized Ireland of only twenty-five years ago, as seen through the bewildered eyes of a child. During his detention, Paddy was viciously assaulted and sexually abused by his religious custodians, and within three years his experiences began to result in physical manifestations of trauma. He was taken one night to hospital and left there, never to see his custodians again. So began his long round of hospitals, mainly in the company of old and dying men, while doctors tried to diagnose his condition. This period of his life, during which he was a constant witness to death, culminated in brain surgery at the age of ten – by which time he had become permanently disabled.

THE GOD SQUAD is the remarkable true story of a survivor, told with an extraordinary lack of bitterness for one so shockingly and shamefully treated. In Paddy Doyle's own words: 'It is about a society's abdication of responsibility to a child. The fact that I was that child, and that the book is about my life, is largely irrelevant. The probability is that there were, and still are thousands of "mes".'

0 552 13582 6

A SELECTION OF FINE AUTOBIOGRAPHIES AND BIOGRAPHIES AVAILABLE FROM CORGI AND BLACK SWAN

THE PRICES SHOWN BELOW WERE CORRECT AT THE TIME OF GOING TO PRESS. HOWEVER TRANSWORLD PUBLISHERS RESERVE THE RIGHT TO SHOW NEW RETAIL PRICES ON COVERS WHICH MAY DIFFER FROM THOSE PREVIOUSLY ADVERTISED IN THE TEXT OR ELSEWHERE.

All Corgi Books are available at your bookshop or newsagent, or can be ordered from the following address:

Corgi/Bantam Books,
Cash Sales Department,
P.O. Box 11, Falmouth, Cornwall TR10 9EN

UK and B.F.P.O customers please send a cheque or postal order (no currency) and allow £1.00 for postage and packing for one book, an additional 50p for the second book, and an additional 30p for each subsequent book ordered to a maximum charge of £3.00 (7 books plus).

Overseas customers, including Eire, please allow £2.00 for postage and packing for the first book plus £1.00 for the second book and 50p for each subsequent title ordered.

Name: (Block Letters) ....

Address: ....

....